Praise for Exploratory Writing

It's a simple question but a profound one: what if we saw the blank page as a space for exploring ideas rather than simply expressing them? Anyone who writes regularly knows that writing is a powerful tool for thinking. This book makes that magic accessible to everyone, at any time. Read it – and prepare to take notes!

Daniel H. Pink, #1 New York Times best-selling author of *The Power of Regret, Drive* and *A Whole New Mind*

Jones reveals a nearly magical cognitive secret: our thinking is made clearer and better via the practice of exploratory writing, which is easy to employ and of great value.

Robert Cialdini, author of *Influence* and *Pre-Suasion*

This is more than a brilliant book about writing; it's a comprehensive toolkit that expands the way we think and create. The book is full of multiple and illuminating insights that anyone could learn from, from those who are thinking about writing through to seasoned authors. It's THE compendium for writers. Outstanding.

Jonathan MacDonald, change expert, speaker and author of *Powered by Change*

It is rare to meet someone that can make a profound difference to how you think. Alison is one of these people. Her message is very powerful and effective. *Exploratory Writing* provides the strategy, the tools and the magic to drive your creativity.

Chris Griffiths, best-selling author of *The Creative Thinking Handbook*

Alison Jones's *Exploratory Writing* is a gem of a book, helping to bring to life the reason why writing can be such a salutary activity for business people, especially in these complex, fast-changing and perturbed times. Aside from ascribing value and benefit to the skill of handwriting (yes, with pen and paper), Jones sets out why and how, in the most practical and pragmatic of ways, to set aside on a regular basis a short amount of time to write. Not only is *Exploratory Writing* good for business, it's good for the soul.

Minter Dial, award-winning author, filmmaker and
international professional speaker

Infused with equal parts scientific research, unique tips, and humor, this brilliant book is an invitation to go deeper in our private inner worlds to be able to better change our outer one.

Molly Beck, CEO of Messy.fm and author of *Reach Out*

Alison Jones makes a great case for exploratory writing as a fresh way of opening up thinking about a whole range of issues – and acting on them. I've just used one of her many practical exercises myself, to help me over a writing block. Enjoyable as well as helpful.

Tom Schuller, author of *The Paula Principle*

A blank sheet of paper is intimidating. It usually inspires a sense of obligation rather than joy. That's why students say 'I must finish my thesis' rather than 'I can't wait to finish my thesis.' It's why guests say 'I have to write this thank you letter', and it's why professional writers say, 'I've got to meet this deadline'. After all, writer's block is the only form of mental paralysis triggered by nothing more than an unused sheet of A4.

Alison Jones stands all this firmly on its head. In *Exploratory Writing*, she sees a blank page as an opportunity to create an adrenalin rush of ideas, a way of opening a door in your imagination. I don't agree with all of it (that would make for a very dull book, wouldn't it?) but I do agree with much of it: and all of it is stimulating, fresh and original.

Roger Mavity, creative guru and writer, author of
Life's a Pitch and *How to Steal Fire*

An inspirational book from an inspirational person. It brims with wisdom and practical advice. This book won't just make you more confident and assured at work, it will make you more confident and assured at living. Alison shows us the importance of writing as a vital means to grow and learn and find our path.

Charlie Corbett, author of *The Art of Plain Speaking* and
12 Birds to Save Your Life

This is a book that I will be referring to on a regular basis. Alison does a great job of making the case for exploratory writing, and most importantly, includes a wealth of practical and creative ways to do it. This book is relevant whether you're new to this kind of writing, or just want some fresh ideas and inspiration. The explanations are clear, and the exercises are both enjoyable and insightful. Highly recommended!

Felicity Dwyer, author of *Crafting Connection*

Many people think they have a book in them but never actually start writing. This interesting approach will help everybody see the joy of freewriting just for pleasure and perhaps it might even get you started on that book too.

Harriet Kelsall, Founder and Chair of Harriet Kelsall Bespoke Jewellery, NED for the British Hallmarking Council and the IPO and author of the award-winning
The Creative's Guide to Starting a Business

This is an empowering and inspiring read. Exploratory writing is a skill that Alison makes accessible, perfect for anyone who wants to supercharge their thinking and do their best work.

Julia Pimsleur, Founder of Million Dollar Women and author of *Million Dollar Women* and *Go Big Now*

I totally love the idea of this book, because it's so absolutely true – writing stuff down really does help you to think more clearly.

Rachel Bridge, former Enterprise Editor of
The Sunday Times and author of eight books including
How to Start a Business without Any Money,
Ambition and *Already Brilliant*

Finally, a book that addresses 'paralysis by analysis' with a practical approach to get started AND compelling theory to counter those 'but what if' objections! Seeing the tabula rasa as an opportunity rather than writer's block, Jones addresses how you think, how what you think can hold you back and, with that, takes away every excuse you might have to get started. It's something all my students – and any procrastinators – need to read with pen and paper at the ready!

Dr Audrey Tang, chartered psychologist and author of
The Leader's Guide to Mindfulness

This is an empowering and uplifting book: such a simple idea, yet the impact is extraordinary. We so often find ourselves reacting rather than responding, feeling hurt without understanding why, or baffled by other people's reactions. Taking time to explore what's going on underneath the surface in a safe space can change everything, for the better.

Alice Sheldon, creator of Needs Understanding and author of
Why Weren't We Taught This at School?

An invitation into a more creative, playful relationship with writing that's hard to resist. So often we spend our days consuming other people's content – this is a reminder that if we simply carve out a little time and space, we too can become creators. Empowering and enjoyable stuff.

Uri Bram, CEO at The Browser and author of
Thinking Statistically

With imagination and levity, this book brings together a practical toolkit of ways to use writing for greater self-understanding. Wherever you're lacking clarity, *Exploratory Writing* renders you the expert in your own life – helping you uncover answers for everyday challenges in life and work.

Megan C. Hayes, PhD, psychologist, author of
The Joy of Writing Things Down and *Write Yourself Happy*

So often the most powerful ideas are the simplest. Alison Jones reminds us of the inexhaustible, unlimited potential of the blank page, at a time when we need a safe space to express ourselves and explore our ideas, without judgement, more than ever. This is a refreshing read, but more than that, it has the potential to make life and work better for its readers

Greg McKeown, author of the New York Times bestseller
Essentialism and *Effortless*

With wisdom and warmth, Alison Jones shows you how to unleash the life-changing magic of exploratory writing. At first glance it appears to be simply a wonderful book about creativity and building a writing habit: once you finish it, you may realize that its true mission was to change the way you look at yourself, your work, and the world.

A. Trevor Thrall, PhD, author of *The 12-Week Year for Writers*

Friendly and fascinating, this book is an invigorating exploration of how writing can offer us a safe space to work through our ideas, tackle our anxieties and truly be creative on the page. Everyday magic, indeed, and a helpful reminder that we can write for ourselves as much as for our readers.

Cathy Rentzenbrink, best-selling author of
The Last Act of Love, Everyone is Still Alive and *Write It All Down*

They say you don't really understand something until you can explain it to someone else. But what if you can't yet explain it to yourself? What Alison has done with this book is given everyone the power to explain any idea to themselves – even if that idea is brand new. A simple but brilliant superpower.

Tom Cheesewright, applied futurist and author of *High Frequency Change* and *Future-proof Your Business*

Many of us have noticed how jotting our thoughts down can help to soothe our mind and sharpen our ideas when we're faced with a challenge – and in this book Alison Jones beautifully demonstrates just how powerful and accessible the technique of exploratory writing can become in our day-to-day lives. With practical guidance and warm encouragement, she shows us an effective, endlessly flexible tool for doing better, feeling better and being better. Wonderful stuff.

Caroline Webb, author of *How to Have a Good Day*

This is a deceptively simple book: it's short and easy to read, but the ideas in it have the potential to change your life. Those of us who write have always understood that it's a tool for thinking as much as for communicating, and now Alison has made this secret available and accessible to everyone, whether they think of themselves as a writer or not. Read it and be inspired!

Robin Waite, business coach and author of *Take Your Shot* and *Online Business Startup*

When you're facing uncertainty – which is most of us, most of the time – writing can be a powerful tool for understanding and personal growth. In this book, Alison Jones shows us how to embrace the life-changing power of the blank page!

Dorie Clark, Wall Street Journal bestselling author of *The Long Game* and executive education faculty, Duke University Fuqua School of Business

Alison's work is a constant source of light and inspiration – this is no exception.

Sam Conniff Allende, author of *Be More Pirate*

So simple, yet so powerful. Pick up your pen and embark on the adventure of exploratory writing, with this book as your companion.

Anne Janzer, author of *The Writer's Process*

A practical book with a profound message that the simplest of practices are often the most important if we are to live with intention and thrive – not just survive – in a world of overwhelm and anxiety.

Simon Alexander Ong, author of *Energize*

When I was a journalist, I used writing as a way of testing ideas and putting them into a coherent pattern. Alison Jones describes this kind of 'exploratory writing' with passion and truthfulness. It is a deeply thought and beautifully written book. Highly recommended.

John Howkins, author of *Invisible Work*

This book has profound implications for any writer. Stop fearing the blank page and get started with a simple practice of exploratory writing that will transform your life on and off the page. Packed full of practical tips – shared with enthusiasm and rigour – it is the perfect companion to deepen your critical thinking. Alison Jones will guide your life in ways you wouldn't expect.

Bec Evans, author of *Written* and *How to Have a Happy Hustle*

I was moved by Alison's book. *Exploratory Writing* made me rethink the role that writing played in my life – a really powerful book.

Bruce Daisley, author of *The Joy of Work* and *Fortitude*

This is such an enjoyable and uplifting read. So vividly written, with riveting stories, fascinating references and packed full of practical tools. I have often noticed how talking about something can deepen my understanding of what I really think and feel; *Exploratory Writing* does the same for the process of writing. It's a fresh and very relatable take on the 'magic' that writing can bring for us all. A brilliant book, as you'd expect from the brilliant Alison Jones.

Rita Clifton CBE, Chair, speaker and
author of *Love Your Imposter*

Exploratory Writing shows us that a humble notepad and pen are often all we need to help us gain a deeper understanding of our complex brains, our work and everything in between. Bursting with clarity and wisdom, this book has brought new perspectives and an invigorating sense of adventure to my writing. Thank you and bravo, Alison.

Graham Allcott, author of *How to be a Productivity Ninja* and
Work Fuel

Health warning for budding authors: THIS BOOK WILL LEAVE YOU EXCUSELESS.

Andy Cope, author of *The Art of Being Brilliant*

Exploratory Writing

Everyday magic for life and work

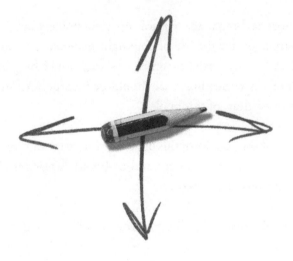

Alison Jones

First published in Great Britain by Practical Inspiration Publishing, 2023

© Alison Jones, 2023

The moral rights of the author have been asserted

ISBN   9781788603676 (print)
          9781788603690 (epub)
          9781788603683 (mobi)

Every effort has been made to trace copyright holders and to obtain their permission for the use of copyright material. The publisher apologizes for any errors or omissions and would be grateful if notified of any corrections that should be incorporated in future reprints or editions of this book.

Want to bulk-buy copies of this book for your team and colleagues? We can customize the content and co-brand *Exploratory Writing* to suit your business's needs.

Please email info@practicalinspiration.com for more details.

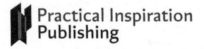

To my fellow explorers:
George, who taught me about paths,
Sorcha, my micro-adventure companion, and
Catherine and Finlay, my two most wonderful and surprising
explorations.

Contents

Foreword

Explore questions to your answers. Alison Jones explains and exemplifies how we can experiment with exploratory writing. In a very accessible style she gives essential background, how to start and lots of tempting ways of moving forward. Exploratory writing only needs everyday tools in our everyday working kit: pencil and paper, perhaps a computer. And it need take very little time: sometimes only six minutes. It is a deceptively simple process: after all, we've all been writing and reading since we were little. So straightforward, yet giving access to so much.

Writing personally and privately in this way can illuminate and significantly develop our lives and work. It does this by opening up strategies for gaining access to hitherto hidden and inaccessible parts of our understanding and memories. This process gives us insight: sometimes quite startling and life-changing insight. Once we begin to explore this much wider and deeper world, we realize how much we've been missing. It's as though we've been living and working in a corridor without even realizing there are windows and doors on either side. More than that: writing enables us to open the window blinds, undo the catches, lean out and look, smell, hear, touch, taste adventure. We can climb out of those windows. Writing can give us the keys to open those doors: explore what's on the other side.

Exploratory writing is accessible at any time, and can be the best possible free coach. Alison tells us: 'a good coach is less about providing answers and much more about asking great questions to help you understand an issue better and create your own solutions'. With our own personal private writing coach, we are always supported and guided towards our own strategies for creating those solutions. The solutions themselves, of course, lead to more questions and more exploring and yet more dynamic possible and potential solutions. Your colleagues and clients will find themselves in new worlds with you.

Alison also reminds us: 'successful people ask better questions'. Successful people are willing to learn how to take responsibility to ask better questions. They are willing to question themselves, their motives and their values, deeply. To the less successful person, this process can seem psychologically dangerous. But as the best coaches would tell you: it is the only route to better solutions. The best coaches help us to be tough on ourselves.

Exploratory writing enables us to look underneath, around, above and beyond issues in our lives which we have hitherto been unable to question. We can gain insight and clarity by perceiving from others' perspective; reflecting on assumptions which we'd misunderstood to be truths; transforming negative emotions such as anger into constructive energy; and learning how to live according to our values more fully. Writing has the power to explore the roots of our work and transform our lives, by questioning our very questions themselves.

Dr Gillie Bolton, author of *Reflective Practice:*
Writing and Professional Development

Introduction

*T*hink about the last journey you took. How much actual exploration did it involve?

For most of us, most of the time, our journeys are hardly polar expeditions. We commute to work, do the school run, visit friends and family, sometimes – not nearly often enough – visit new places on holiday with the benefit of travel guides and sat nav.

It can feel as though our world is fully mapped, that there's little space for exploration and little time for it in any case.

But sometimes we find ourselves exploring the territory rather than just passing through it. On my run each day I take great pleasure in finding new routes, taking paths just to see where they end up, finding unexpected things along the way (a peacock enclosure, an overgrown sculpture, a deconsecrated church…). And it's fascinating too to see how paths join up and intersect, to find new ways of reaching familiar places.

Sure, it'd be nice to be backpacking in the Andes, but most days that's not an option; it doesn't mean I can't have a daily micro-adventure.

And this is also true for mental adventures. I love the buzz of creative workshops and strategy retreats, but most days I just have to turn up and do the work.

This book is about bringing an exploratory mindset to everyday life and work, carving out a few minutes in the day to be explorers rather than exist-ers.

Why? Well, three reasons.

1. It's fun. Which is a great place to start.
2. We live in a world that is changing so fast that it's dangerous for us to approach it with any other mindset.
3. We have an inbuilt tendency to miss what's in front of us and see what we want to see. That means our reactions are often at best unhelpful, and at worst damaging, for ourselves and others. It also means we miss out on opportunities and insights on a daily, maybe hourly, basis.

When we go exploring in a new place, we often do so as part of an expedition organized by someone else – that's how I first discovered the Australian outback, and big fun it was too. In the same way, when we embark on cognitive exploration – creative thinking, problem solving, emotional intelligence exercises, visioning and so on – it's often in the company of an expert who facilitates and guides the work.

Which is great… right up to the point where they leave the room and you're left to carry on the work yourself.

The good news is that once you have the right mindset and a few techniques under your belt, exploratory writing, the kind of writing you'll be discovering in this book, is a way of accessing that big-thinking, workshopping, creative zone whenever you feel like it. And even, sometimes, when you don't.

In a sense, an exploratory writing habit is a complement to any self-development tool you've ever learned, or any you'll ever learn from now on. An exploratory writing session gives you immediate access to your own personal workshop – or even retreat – wherever and whenever you need it.

How I discovered exploratory writing (or how it discovered me)

Before we go any further, let me tell you how I discovered for myself the extraordinary power of exploratory writing, completely by accident.[1]

One night not long after I'd left the corporate world to start my own business, when the cashflow was looking particularly precarious, I woke up in a cold sweat in the small hours. At three o'clock in the morning, a cashflow challenge feels like the start of the collapse of your life. My heart was racing; my throat was tight; I felt giddy, hot and clammy. If I had a rational thought at all, it was simply this: '*What have I done?*'

In this state of wordless panic, doing nothing was impossible so I did what occurred to me: I grabbed a pad of A4 paper and I started to write. It was a hot mess – a howl on paper. But then I started to write about what I was noticing in my body, exactly how the panic felt, where I was feeling it. And as I wrote, I could feel my state changing – my thoughts started slowing down to the pace of my pen on the page, my breathing steadied, I started to feel more centred and calmer.

And that would have been enough, honestly.

But as I wrote, something even more remarkable happened: I had an idea. I found myself writing 'I wonder if…', and after a few minutes, I had a pretty much fully worked-out plan for a new programme, which I launched a couple of weeks later and which helped to solve the cashflow issue.

In just over five minutes that raw, messy writing had allowed me to turn my anxiety around and to access my own resourcefulness and wisdom. And now I was asking: '*What just happened?*'

What had happened was that I'd discovered for myself the power of exploratory writing – writing just for me, not for anyone else. Writing when I didn't even know what it was I wanted to say. It started by simply getting my thoughts onto paper, but in the process it unlocked ideas and insights I hadn't seen before and helped me make sense of the confusion, resourcing me to deal with it more effectively.

Over the next few weeks, I experimented with sitting down and writing in this way every time I felt uncertain or anxious about something or didn't know how to answer a question. And it worked. Every. Single. Time. I felt like I'd discovered the Hogwarts Room of Requirement – it's always there when you need it, it's filled with whatever it is you need at that moment, but most people don't know it exists.

As Harry Potter soon realized with the Room of Requirement, though, just because it was new to me didn't mean I was the first to discover it. People from a wide range of backgrounds have stumbled upon this and written about it: creative writing teachers, therapists, psychologists, learning specialists and others. But very, very few business people.

This book is intended to put that right. If you're a leader or an entrepreneur, or frankly anyone dealing with modern work life, exploratory writing is one of the most flexible and lightweight tools at your disposal for sensemaking, creativity, collaboration, managing stress and overwhelm, and communicating more effectively.

In this book I'm consciously focusing on everyday life and work: if you want to learn how to use writing to address trauma or mental illness, there are many books written by more qualified specialists listed in the bibliography that will help.

But if you're grappling with everyday frustrations – you're in the right place. I hope that you too will discover the freedom and possibilities of the blank page, the excitement of starting a sentence when you have no idea how it's going to end, and the subversive creative joy of being able to write *anything* because nobody's watching.

Since I first stumbled across the power of exploratory writing for myself, I've developed a more explicit methodology together with prompts and tools that make it easier to teach to others, but in essence this is an off-road, off-grid adventure: how you 'do' exploratory writing is entirely up to you. Experiment, see what works, have fun. There are precious few opportunities for ripping up the rule book in modern life, so – you're welcome.

Remember that it was in the Room of Requirement that Harry taught his fellow students the advanced wizarding techniques they needed to overcome the threats they faced – your wand may be an HB pencil or a cheap biro, but it's none the less powerful for that. It can conjure up solutions to some of the most difficult problems we face as humans today: overwhelm, distraction, self-doubt on the one hand and unwarranted self-confidence on the other; lack of empathy for others and ourselves; and an inability to see others' points of view or alternative interpretations of events.

It's a big claim, and in the pages ahead I'm going to do my best to back it up.

But honestly, if you were to close this book now having understood that simply writing when you don't know what it is you want to say is a great way of discovering New Things, and start using that in your everyday life, I'd be a happy author.

(But don't. There's some really good stuff coming up.)

Let's look more closely at this everyday magic. How have humans used it in the past? Why does it work? How can YOU use it to make life and work better?

Exploriamus!

Part 1

Discovering exploratory writing

*T*his first section gets us started with an overview of the terrain:

Chapter 1: what does it mean to 'rediscover' the page?
Chapter 2: what's the science behind this – why should you even try it?
Chapter 3: given that you already know how to write, what does it mean to become an explorer of the page?

And finally, Chapter 4 explores why, in the context of the crisis at work, any of this matters.

Chapter 1

(Re)discovering the page

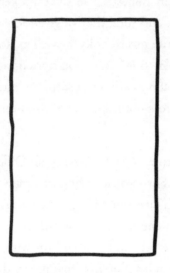

I t's not exactly cutting edge, this, is it, Alison? I've been writing for years now...

If you're in business, you probably do quite a bit of writing. You write emails, sales copy, reports, executive summaries, blog posts, operations documents, memos and more. And each time you write, you're seeking to inform and/or influence your reader. You are, in effect, performing.

What I'm hoping to do here is to get you to see writing in a completely different way. Rather than a public performance space, I want you to see the blank page as uncharted terrain, as an opportunity for you to explore what you DON'T know, rather than simply expressing what you DO.

When I started The Extraordinary Business Book Club podcast back in 2016, my intention was to go under the hood of the business-book-writing process (as much for my own benefit as my listeners', if I'm honest). I've since spoken to hundreds of successful authors, and sure, they've given lots of super-practical tips on how to write great books, as well as how to market and leverage those books. But I very soon started to notice something I hadn't expected: almost without exception, each of them said, in effect, that they wrote not primarily to communicate, but to help them think.

Dave Coplin, former Chief Envisaging Officer at Microsoft, put it like this: 'When you're trying to create something, when you're trying to change something, when you're trying to think differently about something, writing for me is the way that you unravel the spaghetti… and you end up with some really clear, precise thinking that is actionable, that moves the thing forward.'[1]

Dan Pink, author of multiple New York Times bestsellers, said much the same: 'Writing is a form of figuring it out. And in fact for me, sometimes it's essential. It's like, "What do you think about this?" "I don't know, I haven't written about it yet."'[2]

And author and book coach Cathy Rentzenbrink put it this way: 'Writing provides a space in which you can spend quite a lot of time working out for yourself what it is you think and feel about things before there's any temptation or obligation to share those opinions with other people.'[3]

Some authors took this even further: they didn't just write to clarify their thinking, they told me, but to go further upstream, into the murky area of pre-verbal thought – impressions, sensations, ideas.

Coach and author Michael Neill probably put it most poetically: '[Writing] forces me to give form to the formless... it makes me put words to the music. Then you've got a song... I can live it and then when I put words to it I can see it, and then as quickly as possible I want to forget the words and go back to living it. It's richer on the other side for having written it.'[4]

So it's clear that many people who write books see the process of writing as being just as much about thinking as it is about communicating, if not more so.

But are they right? It's time to look at the science behind the magic – what's going on in our brains when we engage in exploratory writing?

Chapter 2
The science behind the magic

To understand why exploratory writing is worth your time and energy – why it works, if you like – we need to engage in a little light neuroscience. If we understand better how our brains function, it's easier to see how we can use exploratory writing to support its more helpful tendencies and to mitigate those that are less helpful.

I believe there are four key neurological dimensions to exploratory writing that make it so damn effective for making life and work better:

- It can function as an **external hard drive** to expand our brain's capacity without distracting it from the work that matters.
- It allows us to **join up and regulate** the different response areas of our brain.
- It allows us to exploit the phenomenon of **instinctive elaboration**, a quirk of our brains that means questions can produce extraordinary results.
- It allows us to unleash our brain's secret weapon – **storytelling** – in the service of sensemaking.

An external hard drive

This aspect of the neurological basis of writing is foundational because it's the reason that it exists at all: the very earliest forms of writing were essentially external hard drives to expand the brain's capacity. Our brains, or if you prefer, 'wetware', are incredibly complex systems; they are flexible and creative, far more advanced than any technology we can currently devise, but they do have limitations. Their storage capacity is finite (opinions vary, but research suggests we can typically keep only three to five items in our working memory[1]) and individually, of course, they are vulnerable to damage, decay and death.

Language, and specifically writing, is what has allowed humans to overcome these limitations and become the world-dominators we are. When we discovered how to write things down, we transcended the limits of our own brains. We could perform complex mathematical operations, create legal systems, organize ourselves beyond the kinship group level to coordinate activity such as city building and international trade, not to mention waging war.

But as Yuval Noah Harari points out in *Sapiens*, once you start accumulating written information, you very quickly need to develop ways of managing it. Without retrieval systems – catalogues, indexing, archives – that allow you to re-find a document when it's needed, it might as well not exist.

Our brain's carbon-based retrieval system is no model for the Library of Congress. It's a mess in there. Harari gives a brilliantly relatable example:

> In the brain, all data is freely associated. When I go with my spouse to sign on a mortgage for our new home, I am reminded of the first place we lived together, which reminds me of our honeymoon in New Orleans, which reminds me of alligators, which remind me of dragons, which remind me of *The Ring of the Nibelungen*, and suddenly, before I know it, there I am humming the Siegfried leitmotif to a puzzled bank clerk. In bureaucracy, things must be kept apart. There is one drawer for home mortgages, another for marriage certificates, a third for tax registers, and a fourth for lawsuits. Otherwise, how can you find anything?[2]

Yes, we need separate, clearly labelled drawers for things if others are to be able to find them. (Or even ourselves, a few months on from when we first stashed them.)

But this bureaucracy, while a necessary coping mechanism for an externalized brain, can't help but shape the way we allow ourselves to think onto paper. Because we're used to writing in a way that others will understand, we automatically play by the bureaucratic rules to which our particular culture subscribes. We stay on topic. We signpost our argument with headings and subheadings and helpful relationship-establishing phrases such as 'This clearly shows that…' or 'Nevertheless…'. We stop regularly to ensure we're still making sense, and that our readers are still with us. And if a tempting side road emerges, we usually resist it – it will only confuse things.

The cranium forms a dividing line. Inside, it's a hot mess of freely associated connections; outside, as we prepare to present our thoughts to others, we tidy things up into compartments and establish logical connections.

Exploratory writing offers an intriguing interface between the two, allowing the shapeless, invisible cognitive anarchy we usually keep inside our skulls out into the world in a safe, private space where we can take a good look at it. It's an invaluable staging post between what we sense at a pre-verbal level and what we ultimately go on to communicate to others.

To stretch the bureaucracy metaphor to breaking point, exploratory writing is the 'in-tray' into which random items are delivered any old how from the Postroom of the Unconscious, ready for the Clerk of Reason to come and sort them out.

(Except that this in-tray is more of a Petri dish: the thoughts grow or combine in new and interesting ways while they wait to be processed. And sometimes it turns out they're too weak to live, and they die quietly. Which is also fine.)

But aren't we awash with modern solutions to this problem, you might ask? We have a multitude of external storage and retrieval systems to support our brains, all of them much smarter than an old-school in-tray. Almost everyone alive today uses technology to supplement their cognitive capacity: we organize our days with online calendars, to-do lists and smart assistants; we access information through search tools rather than committing it to memory; and we communicate and collaborate with others using sophisticated asynchronous tools.

Absolutely. And these technological tools were developed and intended to support our thinking and mental processing, just as writing was so many thousands of years ago.

The difference is that the screen, unlike the page, has turned against us. Our shiny new tech tools are sabotaging us at least as much as they're supporting us. The pings and dings that remind us of a new calendar event or signal a new Slack message interrupt what Cal Newport calls the 'deep work' that we really want to be doing, the very work that those tools were created to free us up for.[3]

In truth, most of us don't even need a ping or even a ding: we're perfectly capable of interrupting ourselves multiple times an hour to check our screens. I'll be coming on to attention in more detail below, as it's such an important topic, but for now it's worth keeping in mind that the ancient practice of writing on paper may be a more benevolent technology for humans than some of its shinier, more 'advanced' rivals – all the benefits of an external drive with none of the downsides of technology that is trying every second to monetize our attention.

Joining up the brain(s)

We talk about 'the brain' as if it's a single unified entity but of course it's not. In *The Chimp Paradox*,[4] psychologist Steve Peters famously simplified its mind-boggling complexity by identifying three key functions:

> **The Human** – the frontal part of the brain, primarily conscious, which is curious, rational and empathetic, seeking meaning and purpose, and which we like to think is in control at all times.

> **The Chimp** – the more primitive limbic area, driven by emotion and instinct, which is reactive, greedy and lazy, and capable of acting much faster than the Human.

> **The Computer** – the parietal area, which stores the beliefs and behaviours that emerge through the interplay of those two systems in our lived experience, which can be accessed by both the Chimp and Human, and which can be programmed deliberately through habit to help us make better choices.

What this means in practice is that our first thoughts aren't usually our most helpful. The Chimp, primed to respond emotionally and hyperaware of negative cues such as fear, anger and shame, typically reacts faster than the Human. And while the Human can step in to regulate the limbic response, that takes time and effort – and all too often the damage has already been done.

Our Chimp routinely sabotages us with negative self-talk – we lash out when we feel threatened; we convince ourselves we can't do something when we're scared; we procrastinate when there's important work to be done; we mess up when we feel under pressure.

We can't get rid of our Chimps and the fear and negative thoughts that go with them, but we can learn to manage them.

What exploratory writing can do, in neurological terms, is to create a connection between the limbic (Chimp) and the rational

(Human) areas of the brain, helping to move us from a state of high anxiety to one in which we are able to reason more effectively. This is what I discovered at 3am all those years ago, as I wrote myself out of the fight-or-flight stress response and into a more productive, calmer, more creative state.

Angela Duckworth provides an interesting insight into this interplay between the different areas of the brain in her report of a conversation with Colorado-based neuroscientist Steve Maier, in which she asked him to explain 'the neurobiology of hope'.

> Steve thought for a moment. 'Here's the deal in a few sentences. You've got lots of places in the brain that respond to aversive experiences. Like the amygdala… Now what happens is that these limbic structures are regulated by higher-order brain areas, like the prefrontal cortex. And so, if you have an appraisal, a thought, a belief—whatever you want to call it—that says, "Wait a minute, I can do something about this!" or "This really isn't so bad!" or whatever, then these inhibitory structures in the cortex are activated. They send a message: "Cool it down there! Don't get so activated. There's something we can do."'[5]

Writing, as opposed to just thinking, can give us the space and time we need to let these higher-order brain areas do their thing and regulate our panicky Chimp, making us more hopeful, and happier, people.

Instinctive elaboration

What did you have for lunch yesterday?

Just for a few nanoseconds there, you had to stop reading because that question hijacked your brain. You just wasted a tiny part of your life you'll never get back recalling yesterday's lunch. Why? Because of a fascinating mental reflex known as 'instinctive elaboration'.[6]

When it's asked a question, your brain can't help but come up with answers. It can be a good question, or a bad, pointless question: instinctive elaboration doesn't distinguish between the two. Most of the time we're barely conscious of the questions we're constantly asking ourselves: exploratory writing makes them more visible, which helps us get smarter about them. Which is important because dumb questions usually generate dumb answers.

If you ask yourself a question like 'Why am I so disorganized?' you'll come up with lots of answers, and they're probably all going to be more or less unhelpful.

If you make that question smarter and ask yourself 'What's one thing I could do today to be more organized?', *then* you're going to get somewhere. This principle is an essential foundation of exploratory writing because when your thoughts are going round in pointless circles, you can hijack your own brain simply by writing a good question as the prompt for an exploratory writing session.

I once took our dog Sorcha, an easily distracted springer spaniel/ border collie cross, on a gundog training course, where one of the lessons was on retrieval. The instructor stood at a distance with the dummy to be retrieved and dropped it into the grass. My job was to crouch alongside Sorcha and point with my arm to show her the direction she was to take to find the dummy. Once I was sure she was lined up right, I released her with a 'Go get it!', and watched as she ran straight to the spot. (It took a bit longer to get her to bring it back, of course, but that's out of scope for this metaphor.) The point is that a good prompt question, when chosen consciously and written at the top of a sheet of paper, acts in a similar way, lining your distractable brain up right and unleashing it in the direction of useful answers.

After all, if we're going to have mental reflexes, we might as well use them, right?

The storytelling brain

Just as we aren't usually conscious of the questions we're asking in the privacy of our own heads, we're often unaware of the stories we're telling ourselves there too. We tend to think of narrative as something that's the province of novelists and screenwriters, but at the most fundamental level, we're all born storytellers. The only way we can process our experience and create sense is through constructing stories, consciously or subconsciously. We tell ourselves stories from the moment we wake up to the moment we go to sleep – and even after that: we're so wired to process the world narratively that we do it in our sleep ('dreaming' is just another word for 'involuntary storytelling').

Right now your brain is engaged in reading this and following my argument (I hope). But if you were to put this book down for a moment and go make yourself a cup of tea – try it, you know you want to – you'd find your brain would quickly switch back to its default mode: chattering away to itself, telling more or less inconsequential stories. The 'auto-biographical self' takes over in the absence of anything better to do.[7]

Through stories we rehearse life events and integrate learning. Stories allow us to store more Stuff by creating more complex neural pathways (a 1969 study showed that when we hear items presented narratively rather than in a simple list, our long-term recall increases by a factor of up to 7).[8] Stories are maps that allow us to navigate the world, and we simply can't operate without them.

But stories can also be problematic because we start to believe the stories we create, to confuse them with the world as it really is. We want to see patterns, to create certainty. When our emotional brain makes a decision, our rational brain scrambles to make sense of it by creating a story that fits, and we call this 'truth'.

It's like the old joke about the fish:

> There are these two young fish swimming along, and they happen to meet an older fish swimming the other way, who nods at them and says, 'Morning, boys. How's the water?' And the two young fish swim on for a bit, and then eventually one of them looks over at the other and goes, 'What the hell is water?'[9]

Here we are, in company with our chattering, storytelling brains, thoughts scudding past at the speed of, well, thought. That's our water. That chattering, those stories – we don't even notice them most of the time, and when we do, we take them for truth. 'This is what's happening,' we tell ourselves. 'This is how the world is.'

But of course our only access to the world is through our perception and thoughts. Ask two people to tell you about the same event and you'll hear two very different stories. In such a situation you would be an observer who could assess the relative 'truth' of those stories, understand why one person responded as they did, perhaps see both sides. But we're not dispassionate observers of our own experience.

Exploratory writing allows us to step out of the water for a moment and observe our own thoughts and perceptions, to see them for what they are – just a way of understanding the world. As Michael Neill puts it: 'We think we are experiencing reality; we are actually experiencing our thinking.'[10]

Exploratory writing can also help us make our stories visible, which is the first step towards deciding whether or not they're helpful. It also allows us to consider new stories, which give us a glimpse of other possibilities, other choices we could make which might lead to different outcomes. Just as a novelist creates fictional worlds, we can create new possible futures for ourselves on paper, and that act alone can transform our state of mind because it translates into agency.

Of course, I can't do the whole story of writing and neurology justice in one chapter. But I hope this brief introduction has convinced you that exploratory writing can have a powerful impact on our lived experience, and that you're ready to start your own exploration. Before we get going, let's talk about the mindset and the basic kit that we're going to need to take with us.

Chapter 3

Becoming an explorer

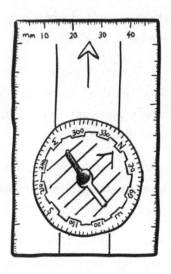

*B*efore an explorer heads off on any expedition, there's some preparation to be done. Granted, you don't need much in the way of specialist equipment or logistical support to tackle a blank page. But as with any form of adventuring, the most important preparation of all is to get your head into the right place for the challenge ahead.

The explorer's mindset

When you sit down to write in the usual course of your work day, you're not typically in exploration mode. You've got a pretty good idea of what you want to communicate before you start writing, and your focus is on how to communicate it clearly and in a way that's most likely to get the response you desire.

It's as if you're at the start line of a race: you know exactly what you have to do, the course is marked out before you, and your job is to complete it as effectively and efficiently as possible. If you can get a metaphorical medal, so much the better.

When you sit down to do some exploratory writing, however, the race mindset is useless. You don't know the route ahead of you; that's the whole point of exploration. So this kind of writing is not about performance, but discovery.

Many people have attempted to identify exactly what the explorer's mindset consists of, but there's general consensus around a few key principles: curiosity, humility, adaptability and humour.

These are vitally important if you're trekking across the Arctic in a blizzard, of course, but they're equally useful in more local challenges: navigating a tricky interpersonal issue at work, for example, or trying to set up a new venture. And they're helpful too in the metaphorical expedition that is exploratory writing.

Let's look at each of them in turn.

Curiosity

If there's a single defining characteristic of an explorer, it must surely be curiosity. Whether the question is 'I wonder what's on the other side of this mountain', 'I wonder if the earth is really flat', or 'I wonder if I've got what it takes to reach the North Pole on roller skates', curiosity lies behind pretty much every explorer's decision to go and explore.

But curiosity does more than just get us started; it's also what allows us to look at the challenges inherent in exploration without running away screaming.

It give us what Grace Marshall calls 'a better way of seeing':

> Fear says, 'Shit! Something's happening!'
>
> Curiosity says, 'Oh! Something's happening!'
>
> Fear says, 'Danger.'
>
> Curiosity says, 'That's interesting!'
>
> Fear says, 'Don't go there.'
>
> Curiosity says, 'Let's take a closer look.'[1]

Most creativity starts with curiosity, and exploratory writing provides a space in which to exercise it on a small-scale, daily basis. Because the page is a safe space, because the stakes are low and there's no risk to life, limb or reputation, it makes it easier for the more helpful curiosity to take control and translate the knee-jerk response of fear into fact-finding, world-expanding exploration.

Humility

This is the foundation of learning: the willingness to entertain the possibility that you might be wrong, that there might be a better way to do things. Paradoxically it's a sign of inner confidence: it's the most insecure people who resist the idea of being wrong most strenuously. Being comfortable with being wrong is at the root of what psychologist Carol Dweck famously called 'growth mindset': those with a fixed mindset find criticism and the success of others threatening, but an individual with a growth mindset sees both as opportunities for learning.[2]

Humility is becoming increasingly important for business leaders because the complexity and pace of change of the modern world mean that no-one can know all the answers all the time. Being humble enough to hold your own beliefs lightly and seek out the opinions of others is essential not just for success but for survival. Approaching exploratory writing with an attitude of humility means being willing to explore other ways of seeing a situation and willing too to learn from others even if you don't much like them.

Edgar Schein coined the term 'humble inquiry', meaning the art of asking questions to which you don't know the answer, with the aim of drawing out and building a relationship with the other person.[3] It's a proven strategy for more effective leadership and better decision-making. In exploratory writing the 'other' is yourself, but the principle is the same: humility is what allows explorers to accept that the reality might be different to what they've imagined, and that they might have to change their plans and even their view of the world in response to what they find.

Adaptability

One characteristic of all expeditions since the dawn of time is that none have gone exactly to plan. It's hardly surprising: almost by definition there can be no firm plan when the territory ahead is unknown. So while explorers prepare as rigorously as possible, they also have to accept that at some point something unforeseen will happen and they'll have to adapt accordingly.

When it became clear that the *Endurance* was about to be crushed by ice, Ernest Shackleton famously turned his exploration mission into a rescue mission and dedicated himself to bringing his men back alive. The day they had to abandon ship and camp on the nearby ice, he wrote in his journal: 'A man must shape himself to a new mark directly the old one goes to ground.'[4] Had he spent his energy cursing his luck or trying to salvage his original plan, there's no way he'd have achieved the remarkable feat of improvisation, adaptability and resilience that ultimately brought them all safely home.

Committing to a change of plan is a significant step, especially if it involves convincing other people to come along. Exploratory writing allows us limitless potential to formulate, test and refine potential alternative plans free from consequences. It also enables us to develop the arguments we'll need to convince others that this new route is worth taking.

Humour

You might not immediately think of humour as an archetypal characteristic of explorers: there's a certain grimness associated with setting your face into the blizzard. But humour is important if people spending a long time together in difficult circumstances aren't to kill each other (Roald Amundsen claimed in his diary in 1911 that his indomitably cheerful cook Adolf Lindstrom 'rendered greater and more valuable services to the Norwegian polar expedition than any other man'[5]). And even for solo explorers of the page, humour is a helpful tool to deploy when the going gets tough or things don't go according to plan (*see: Adaptability*). Being able to find humour in a situation, however dark, reduces perceived stress. Humour also puts us into a more creative, playful state, which is where you'll most often find solutions and new ideas. One great benefit of solo exploring is that you don't need to worry about offending anyone else with inappropriate sniggering. So as you set out on your exploratory writing adventure, feel free to acknowledge and embrace absurdity or gallows humour wherever you find it as long as it's helpful (as with any kind of humour, when it tips into cruelty, it stops being funny).

As you set out on your exploratory writing journey, it's worth keeping the principles of curiosity, humility, adaptability and humour in mind. If you make a conscious choice to adopt them from the beginning, they'll become habitual over time. And that could make a huge difference not only in your writing, but in your life.

The explorer's toolkit

As well as equipping yourself metaphorically with the right mindset, there are some more literal items of equipment to assemble before you go adventuring, and some instructions to keep in mind.

Wait a minute, you might be saying – I thought the whole point of exploratory writing was that you only need a pen and a piece of paper, and that it's impossible to do it wrong? So why do I need an equipment list and instructions?

To which the answer is: yes, in one sense, there's nothing complicated about exploratory writing. There isn't a 'right' way and a 'wrong' way to do it. But there *are* some helpful tools and ideas, and some core skills which will make your practice not only more useful but more fun.

Just as you wouldn't go on any expedition without basic supplies – first-aid kit, sleeping bag, tent, boots, peanut butter (or maybe that's just me) – so there are a few things you can't do without when it comes to exploratory writing. They're not exactly specialist equipment...

What do you need?

- A pen or pencil.
- A big scruffy pad of paper (more on this below).
- Somewhere comfortable to write.
- Some way of timing yourself.
- No distractions – from people or devices – during that time.

What else might you like?

- A nice notebook for capturing insights/actions in a more presentable way.
- Tea. And maybe a biscuit.

When do you do it?

Whenever you damn well like. First thing in the morning is good, mostly because it helps you set the direction for your day before everyone else starts trying to get a piece of you. Evening is also good as a way of reflecting on and processing the experiences of the day. But any time you feel the need for a bit of space and clarity is a good time for exploratory writing.

How long do you do it for?

This is a great question. On the one hand, the answer is of course similar to that for *when* you should do it, namely as long as you damn well like. Not every exploratory writing session needs to have a deadline. But I've found a deadline is helpful, not least because it focuses my attention and helps me write more quickly, and speed is one of the best ways of breaking through the invisible barrier between what we know we know and what we don't know we know.

For me, six minutes is about as long as I can keep up a true freewriting sprint, by which I mean writing at the speed of thought without stopping, before my energy – or my hand – drops off.

I started my daily exploratory writing practice with a target of ten minutes and discovered that I failed more often than I succeeded. Ten minutes just seemed more than I could spare on a busy day.

So I reduced my goal to five minutes – *'I don't care how busy you are, Alison, you can find five minutes.'* And I could, most days. Not only that, but the short timescale helped me to focus, to write more quickly and therefore more freely. But the problem is that it takes most people two or three minutes to get going with exploratory writing, which means that if your session is only five minutes long, you only really have two or three minutes for the good stuff. (In this, I find writing is a little like running: the first few minutes are always dreadful.)

And then I read Gillie Bolton's *Reflective Practice*,[6] in which she recommends six minutes as the optimum sprint time, and when I tried it I was converted. Six minutes feels just as doable as five, but you get a whole extra minute of good stuff. It's a high-yield additional investment of 60 seconds.

So while it is *entirely* up to you, I'd strongly recommend you start by setting a timer for six minutes. If when it goes off you want to carry on, that's great. But you don't have to.

How often do you do it?

Again, it's tempting to say as often as you like.

But let me put the argument for consistency. I run every day. I don't run very far most days, and I don't run very fast, ever. But as I write this in July 2022 I've run every day for more than 1,500 days, and I don't plan to stop until circumstances force me to (as one day they inevitably will). Until then, I have a non-negotiable daily habit that makes me happier and healthier (and which the dog loves even more than I do).

Doing something every day is known as 'streaking'. (This has nothing to do with the wearing – or rather not wearing – of clothes. That's a completely different kind of streaking and this is not that kind of book.) I have a number of 'streaks': habits that I've consciously committed to doing daily. Each one reflects an aspect of the person I want to be, physically, mentally, socially and spiritually, and none of them takes too long because otherwise I wouldn't be able to sustain them for the long term.

We know from a vast body of psychological research, such as the work of B. J. Fogg into 'tiny habits'[7] and James Clear's 'atomic habits',[8] that this approach of embedding small changes through regular habits is the best way for most of us to successfully change our lives for the better and to sustain that change.

Once I'd committed to my running streak, something very interesting happened: instead of asking myself 'Am I going to run today?' – to which the answer had all too often in the past been,

'Nah, don't feel like it' – the question I had to ask myself was 'WHEN am I going to run today?' That's a very different decision. It requires a bit of light planning rather than the heavy machinery of willpower. Because I am streaking I am precommitted, and precommitment is one of the smartest tools in our psychological kitbag when it comes to getting stuff done.

If you think that might work for you, I'd encourage you to experiment with an exploratory writing streak. Make sure you have some way of recording it (Jerry Seinfeld famously puts a cross through each day on his wall calendar; I use the Streaks app, you do you). The point is that seeing an unbroken string of days helps to motivate you not to break the chain.

Why a scruffy pad of paper? I've got lots of really nice notebooks...

I love notebooks. I have several on my shelves that are just too beautiful ever to write in: I will never have a thought profound enough or be able to scribe neatly enough to justify spoiling their pristine pages. Nobody needs that kind of pressure here. Exploratory writing is raw and messy and honest, and when you start you need to be sure that nobody else is ever going to see it.

For me, the best vehicle for exploratory writing is a big block of recycled lined A4 paper. It's cheap, it's unintimidating, it's temporary, it's unselfconscious, and it engages both brain and body in a way that a computer keyboard can only dream about.

So a big yes to beautiful notebooks – but save them for capturing the polished, processed insights that emerge from your exploratory writing, rather than for the exploratory writing itself. (More on this in Chapter 14.)

And that's it. It's hardly an onerous or expensive list, and it doesn't demand much from you in the way of time commitment or technical expertise. Even if you find that a particular day's exploratory writing attempt was a dead loss, you've lost nothing more than six minutes and a couple of sheets of paper.

To end this introductory section, I want to take a few moments in the next chapter to focus particularly on the world of work, and why I believe exploratory writing is such a powerful tool as we struggle at all levels of the organization to meet the challenges we face there.

Chapter 4

Exploratory writing and the crisis at work

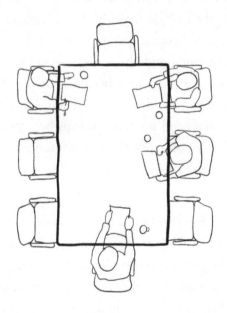

*T*rying to draw an artificial line between life and work is somewhat pointless, but it's worth paying special attention to how exploratory writing might be particularly useful there given that the workplace, real or virtual, is:

- where most of us spend most of our waking hours;
- where we have multiple interactions each day with people we've not necessarily chosen to spend time with;
- where we most like to pretend that our Human is in control;
- currently facing an unprecedented crisis of wellbeing and engagement.

You may feel that 'crisis' is a strong word, but it's hard to argue that things are rosy in the working week.

For a start, there's 'The Great Resignation', a term coined by Professor Anthony Klotz in 2021 to refer to the epidemic of people quitting their jobs in the immediate aftermath of the Covid pandemic.[1] Perhaps because they'd discovered they preferred life without the commute and the office politics; perhaps because they'd had time and space to think more deeply about the big questions of life and decided that their job didn't match up to their broader values and purpose; perhaps because an escalating cost-of-living crisis was making it uneconomic to drive miles to get to their place of work; or perhaps for some other reason entirely.

Then there's the fact that only a small proportion of workers are actively engaged at work (Gallup's estimate for the first half of 2021 was 20% globally, and it's been in that ballpark for years now[2]), spending much of their day on social media rather than the three-year strategy. Even if they're trying to focus on the strategy document, they're likely to be distracted by a productivity-killing DM from the boss or a call from a colleague.

Not to mention the steady increase over the last decade in the incidence of work-related stress,[3] which has been variously attributed to workload, dealing with disruption, and uncertainty.

New anxieties associated with the pace of technological change are overlaying the age-old anxieties associated with difficult relationships and poor leadership and communication.

Businesses spend billions of dollars each year on addressing these issues with change management programmes, executive coaching, leadership training, wellbeing initiatives and so on. But as you'll see in this book, exploratory writing offers benefits that are particularly well suited to these complex pressures – benefits such as engagement, problem solving, resilience and empathy – and at a fraction of the cost.

Not convinced? Let's look at three very practical examples of how an exploratory writing practice can be put to work in the workplace, producing extraordinary results for a tiny investment of time.

'Invisible work' and collaboration

Most of what we do at work these days seems very strange to a pre-digital generation. (My childhood friend's mother sent a Christmas card to my own mother every year until she died. In the last one before her death she wrote matter-of-factly: 'Paul and Ailsa are both well, both doing jobs I don't understand.')

And whereas 'knowledge work' used to be the province of a very few specialist roles, today it encompasses the majority of us. Which means that much of our time at work is spent either trying to make our invisible thoughts visible to others or attempting to 'see' what others are trying to make visible to us. As John Howkins points out, this is not easy: 'Handing over a half-completed idea is tricky.'[4]

Howkins goes on to suggest one way of achieving this from his own experience, working alongside Greg Dyke at the founding of Channel 5. Dyke would write a letter or memo, trying to reduce the complex financial and technical dimensions of the issue at hand into a clear communication, and then a small team would sit around reworking that message and gaining clarity themselves along the way. As he notes: 'it was a good way to bring invisible work out into the open.'[5]

Exploratory writing is an invaluable tool in the work of making the invisible visible, as it gives each member of the team space to 'see' their ideas more clearly before they engage in the work of communicating them to others.

Here is an example of a very practical application of exploratory writing in the workplace: instead of leaping into a collaborative conversation, it can be useful for team members to spend a few minutes at the start of a meeting writing first for themselves. What do they see as the key issues? What are they trying to make their colleagues understand? What possibilities most intrigue them?

Adding in this 'pre-discussion' step is likely to result in a more helpful group discussion, and also to surface concerns and ideas that might otherwise not be seen at all.

Diversity and inclusion

One powerful advantage of using exploratory writing in team situations is that it can help level the playing field: traditional meetings and so-called 'brainstorming' sessions privilege confident, neurotypical, extravert native-language speakers with a preference for an activist rather than reflective learning style. These early contributions can then shape and skew the whole discussion.

Simply allowing a few minutes for everyone to write for themselves, in their own language and according to their own preferences, can surface high-quality ideas from every participant. This can help embed inclusivity and diversity across all dimensions, as well as generating a wider range of ideas for evaluation and allowing those who have traditionally resigned themselves to being on the periphery of the action to become more engaged.

By way of a practical example to show how exploratory writing can be used in this more inclusive way, consider the premortem,[6] a term coined by Gary Klein and popularized by Daniel Kahneman. A post-mortem is useful for understanding the cause of death, but it comes rather too late to be of any use to the object being studied; a premortem invites team members to play a game. Let's assume the project has failed: what might have caused that? This is entirely hypothetical; nobody's reputation is on the line, no-one has skin in the game, so it is easier for people to surface concerns that might otherwise go unspoken. Using a short exploratory writing sprint helps participants to go beyond their immediate ideas to find less obvious potential issues, which are often, of course, the ones that turn out to be the deadliest. It also allows each person to bring their unique areas of insight and expertise to bear on the issue, rather than simply those with the loudest voices and readiest opinions.

Wellbeing at work

Employee wellbeing is a hot topic for leaders, not least because of the impact on organizations. A pre-pandemic report commissioned by the UK government in 2017 found that: 'While there are more people at work with mental health conditions than ever before, 300,000 people with a long-term mental health problem lose their jobs each year, and at a much higher rate than those with physical health conditions... [and] around 15% of people at work have symptoms of an existing mental health condition', and they estimated the annual cost to UK employers to be between £33bn and £42bn.[7] This situation has not been improved by Covid. With one in four people experiencing a mental health problem each year, according to UK charity Mind,[8] it's clear that leaders need to take the wellbeing of their people seriously not just because they want to be decent human beings, but because there are real costs involved if they don't.

I'll talk in more detail about how exploratory writing can support wellbeing in Chapter 11, but for now it's worth noting that the recommendations for employers in the 2017 report include 'encouraging open conversations' about mental health. It's clear that exploratory writing could play a part in enabling that thoughtful, open communication by providing a safe space in which to begin articulating things that are difficult to say out loud.

Part 2

On-page, off-piste adventures

*B*y now I hope that you're on board with this expedition: you understand why it's worth your time and effort, you've adopted the explorer's mindset and you're ready with your basic kit.

It's time to start your adventures in exploratory writing. In this section I'll introduce some of the directions in which you can go – a series of adventures you can take on the page. We'll be looking at:

Chapter 5: agency, intention and attention, the three intertwined principles by which we get anything of significance done at all;

Chapter 6: sensemaking, our constant but often unconscious narrative-construction;

Chapter 7: inquiry, a more purposeful way of using questions;

Chapter 8: playfulness, the foundation of creativity;

Chapter 9: transformation, the extraordinary power of metaphor to help us see things differently;

Chapter 10: self-knowledge, getting comfortable with the aspects of ourselves we usually try to ignore; and

Chapter 11: wellbeing, how we can be better resourced to meet the challenges we face each day.

Feel free to explore at your own pace and start wherever you wish. In most of the chapters in this section you'll find suggested prompts for your exploratory writing adventure marked with a blank page like this. (But they're only suggestions – if you want to use a different prompt or take a different direction, go right ahead!)

Chapter 5
Adventures in agency,
intention and attention

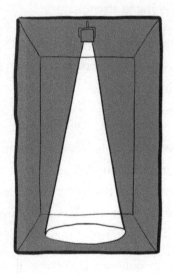

*I*n Chapter 2 we looked at the neurological basis for taking exploratory writing seriously – why it works, if you like. In this chapter, as we begin to look at specific applications for exploratory writing, let's start by shifting our focus from the hardware of the brain to the software of the mind: psychology and philosophy. Or to put it another way, why it matters.

I believe there are three interconnected, foundational principles that underpin the magic of exploratory writing: agency, intention and attention. Like all psychological and philosophical terms they're the subject of vigorous debate, but for the purposes of this book I will define them like this:

Agency = capacity for making things happen, for impacting the world.

Intention = deliberately choosing what, out of the million different things you COULD make happen today, or in your lifetime, you are going to attempt.

Attention = focusing your mind and energy on your chosen priority in a consistent and persistent way in order to make those intended things happen.

These principles are inextricably interdependent: if we believe we have agency, we can bring our intention to deciding what it is we're going to attempt. This means we are more likely to achieve it through sustained attention over however many weeks, months, maybe even years, it takes.

If we don't believe in our own agency, we'll never even try to achieve anything significant. If we don't bring intention to the task of choosing, we'll drift through life. And if we can't marshal our attention to the task we've chosen, we won't see it through. When the three work together they create a virtuous circle: as we see results from focusing our attention on the goals we've chosen to pursue, our sense of our own agency increases.

I call these principles foundational because without them it's impossible for us to achieve anything of real value.

Let's look at each of them in turn to see how exploratory writing can help.

Agency

We saw in Chapter 2 that writing allows us to see our own stories. That separation between ourselves and our thoughts effectively allows us to have some degree of control over them: we can notice the stories we're telling ourselves, assess them and imagine new possibilities; we can make decisions about what to accept and what to reject; we can try out thought experiments.

So much of what happens to us day by day is outside our control, from other people's behaviour to the weather to a cost-of-living crisis. Even if we're not in the grip of truly disempowering circumstances such as illness, poverty, abuse or discrimination, most of us spend much of our time feeling more or less powerless, which is a soul-sucking sort of a state.

Exploratory writing allows us to transform the page into a small and yet infinite space where we can have complete control – we're not answerable to anyone else; we're not constrained by any reality unless we choose to be; we can follow any thought that takes our fancy and imagine any state we choose. You might not feel able to stand up in front of a roomful of people and give a presentation right now, but you can write about doing it, and by authoring that experience you can visualize it in much the same way that an athlete might visualize crossing the finishing line in an Olympic final.

Visualization has been used by sports coaches for decades now: when an athlete mentally rehearses the outcome they want it triggers brain activity similar to the experience itself. The visualization creates a new neural pathway, which primes the athlete to act in a way consistent with that outcome, thereby making it more likely that they'll achieve their goal.[1]

You may not be planning to use this mental magic to win an international sporting event any time soon (I know I'm not), but there's no rule against using it in other areas of your life. Exploring on the page what it would be like to nail that presentation, get that promotion, launch that podcast – whatever it is that you want to achieve, and which seems out of your grasp – can help it feel more possible. And that sense of agency quickly translates into your attitude and behaviour, which can't help but lead to better outcomes.

Exploratory writing creates a space in which we can regain our sense of being in charge of our own experience. Megan Hayes calls this 'self-authoring': she explains that 'the feeling that we can make things happen is a very powerful one, and writing is a simulation of that because we can make things happen on the page, we can make sense of them'.[2]

This can feel a little like magic. Often when someone finishes their first exploratory writing sprint they look at me – slightly dazed – and say 'I don't believe it!'. It's as if they'd just watched themself produce a rabbit from a hat (which, metaphorically, is pretty much exactly what they've done, of course).

The first few times I tried this for myself I thought I'd just got lucky, but once I'd done 20+ writing sprints and come up with something worthwhile every single time, I started to realize I was making my own luck. And that is very confidence inspiring. You, like me, will start to realize that actually you *do* have the answers to the everyday questions and situations that are stumping you: you just needed a page-shaped space and six minutes or so to find them. Which in time makes you feel more able to step up to new, more challenging questions and situations.

Even if we believe ourselves capable of meaningful action, however, the two vital resources we need to bring to the task – intention and attention – are under relentless attack from our modern way of life and work.

Intention

Having established your agency, your capacity to take meaningful action, the obvious question becomes: what action will you take? And since (as hockey star Wayne Gretzky famously pointed out) you miss 100% of the shots you don't take, the act of choosing the shots that you *will* take is of central importance in determining your final outcomes.

Setting an intention requires some conscious thought, and it also demands some courage. It is, after all, much easier *not* to take the shot, as then there's no possibility of failing, with all the embarrassment and uncomfortable sensations that involves. By not setting an intention, you get to sit in the stands with everyone else watching the game. This is a far more comfortable place to be: no risk of failure or injury, and you can munch snacks as you criticize the players for *their* misses.

Setting an intention and acting on it not only involves the possibility of failure; it means deliberately separating yourself from those content to stay in the stands. This is hard, especially if your identity is bound up with theirs. 'Who do you think you are?' we imagine they are saying. 'Sit back down and shut up. This is where you belong, with us. Have another hotdog.'

It's much easier to let someone else set your intentions for you. That's how we're socialized as children at home and in the classroom, after all. We're given chores, and if we perform them well, we are rewarded. In the past, most people were expected to carry that attitude on into working life too. But more and more of us are now classed as 'knowledge workers', working more independently, flexibly and with more autonomy than our production-line-bound predecessors, working outside corporate life altogether as entrepreneurs, or hustling on the side. The importance of setting our own intentions has never been greater.

To complicate matters, the number of options between which we have to choose has never been greater, too. So much choice can be paralysing. If you can be anything, go anywhere, do anything, how do you decide? What if you get it wrong? Relentless social media scrutiny means that failure is more public than ever. All in all, deciding to set your intentions is a risky business. The only thing worse than doing it, in fact, is not doing it.

Once again, exploratory writing provides a safe space in which to formulate and test your intentions. You can use the page as a time machine: what might things look like in five years' time if you take this action? And what if you don't? Or you can run a line down the middle and create a pros-and-cons argument that helps you set out and evaluate the debate going on in your head. Even just seeing a possible course of action set out on paper, having gone through the process of articulating it, can give you a sense that it is achievable.

Attention

If intention is choosing to take a particular shot, attention is the focus we bring to it, both in the moment and in the weeks, months and years of training involved in achieving it. And we appear to be in the middle of an attention crisis.

Part of this is pure FOMO. Choosing to pay attention to one thing means by definition choosing *not* to pay attention to other things, and when there are so many things out there clamouring for our attention, and so much marketing spend invested in trying to persuade us how essential they are to our happiness, that's not easy.

Another part is our addiction – and that's not too strong a word for it – to our devices. I'm sure you've heard the statistics: a 2018 report found that the average smartphone owner interacts with their phone 2,617 times a day,[3] which doesn't leave time for much else, frankly. Our devices and the apps that run on them are designed by some of the smartest minds on the planet to win ever-increasing amounts of our attention and monetize it, so don't feel bad. The odds are stacked against you – it's not you, it's them. Fixing it, though? Until we get some fit-for-21st-century-purpose tech regulation, that's down to you.

A less talked-about component of the attention crisis is the expectations that others have of us. I'm old enough to remember the days of the internal office memo, which would arrive in a buff envelope secured with string wound around a cardboard button. It took a little while to reach its recipient via the office mail cart, and it would take some time for your response to get back too. If you were engaged in something else, you would leave it to one side until you'd finished what you were doing; if it was urgent, they'd have rung or come to see you.

Today, of course, our colleagues can see immediately that we've received and read their message, which creates an unspoken obligation to reply quickly. And so it goes on, with them replying to your reply. You hang up. No, *you* hang up.

So often what we intend to achieve on any given day is hijacked by others' demands and, if we're honest, sometimes we're even grateful. Stevie Smith sat at her desk longing for the person from Porlock, the person who (in)famously interrupted Samuel Taylor Coleridge as he feverishly transcribed his drug-fuelled vision to create 'Kubla Khan': 'I am hungry to be interrupted', she admitted.[4] And aren't we all, sometimes? It gets us off the hook. If no distraction comes along, we have no excuse not to finish that poem, write that report, find that solution. Maybe that's why we are so addicted to checking our phones: we too long for the person from Porlock, and if they're not going to oblige us by showing up at the door, we'll go looking for them on TikTok.

'Inner work' practices such as meditation can be great ways to help us strengthen focus, but they bring their own challenges. Maybe you can sustain a mental state of calm detachment and oneness with the universe for more than 30 seconds: I know I can't.

But I've discovered that even those who, like me, are suckers for distraction and have an abysmal attention span for purely mental work CAN sustain a focused writing sprint for six minutes. There are two (related) reasons for this:

1. **It's offline**. Time spent doing exploratory writing with a pen and paper is effectively time off-grid. Nobody can interrupt us remotely; no app can make its bid for our attention; we can't flick to Google to find the answer to a question and then lose an hour to breaking news or, let's face it, cat videos. Just as importantly, nobody can

track our keystrokes or access a shared document: we can say whatever we like, free from digital spies. If that feels subversive, it's because it is.

2. **It anchors our focus.** Inside our heads, thoughts tend to circle endlessly, and as we can only hold one in front of us at any one time it's hard to keep our attention on an idea long enough to develop it in any significant way, even at the best of times. And when we DO have an insight, any distraction – that incoming message alert, for example – can make it evaporate in a second. Thinking onto paper allows us to unspool our thinking and hold onto the thread, rewind if we need to, come back to the point. Whereas thinking often feels like going round in circles, writing gives us the sense of moving forward.

These might sound like esoteric principles, but a daily exploratory writing practice allows us to embed them into the day-to-day stuff of life. Just for a few minutes each day, it allows us to connect with a sense of our own agency, to practise intention, and to bring our attention to that in a way that quite simply helps us get more of the stuff that matters done.

Chapter 6
Adventures in sensemaking

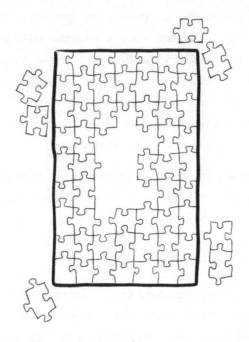

*I*n Chapter 2 we saw that the brain can't help but make a story, and that exploratory writing can help us notice those stories and try out new ones. Stories are the way that we make sense of the world; the wider process by which we construct those stories is known as sensemaking. When we engage in sensemaking we select the elements of experience to which we will pay attention, and we begin to link those experiences relationally: B happened because of A; if X, then Y.

We're used to reading carefully crafted linear narratives in novels, but exploratory writing is looser, more associative, messier – because as we also saw in Chapter 2, that's how our brains work. As Peter Elbow puts it, 'Our habitual thinking is seldom strictly logical but rather associating, analogical, metaphorical.'[1]

So sensemaking is a sort of proto-narrative: it begins simply by noticing and selecting, more or less consciously, what it is we're bringing our attention to. Through the process of exploratory writing we start to create a sense of a 'connected sequence', the associations and analogies that help us get some perspective and try out different interpretations. As Karl Weick observes in his landmark book *Sensemaking in Organizations*, 'When people punctuate their own living into stories, they impose a formal coherence on what is otherwise a flowing soup.'[2]

Much of our sensemaking happens socially, in conversation with others or within the culture of an organization, and typically without much in the way of conscious thought. Our storytelling brains simply translate 'experience' into 'narrative' without any effort or even awareness on our part.

But exploratory writing allows us to make that process visible at the very edge of our awareness, where experience is translated into language and events into narrative. And that allows us to spot the often unhelpful assumptions that underpin them and try out alternatives.

Because our brains are constantly, busily creating stories out of the raw material of our experience, all too often our instinctive sensemaking becomes unhelpful. We slide into rumination

– endless circles of reliving a bad experience, recrimination, blame, regret, anxiety.

Exploratory writing is a way to use this sensemaking habit of our brains more purposefully and playfully. The old circular ruts that we've ruminated around in for so many years are deeply ingrained, and often the only way to break out of them is to get some speed behind us.

This is why freewriting, perhaps the most fundamental tool in the exploratory writing kitbag, is so powerful.

Freewriting

I introduced freewriting briefly back in Chapter 3 as part of the basic toolkit of exploratory writing, but it's time to look at it in more detail, and (you guessed it) give it a try. Freewriting is simply writing whatever is in your head, without editing or censoring, as close as possible to the speed of thought.

It's free of judgement, your own or anyone else's, and if necessary can also be free of grammar, punctuation, any kind of polish or style, and certainly any sense of what's appropriate or 'proper'. It doesn't even need to make sense (although you'll probably be surprised just how much sense it does make when you look back on it). It's free of all the constraints that usually apply to writing that's intended for other people, and it can take some time to get the hang of this dizzying sense of freedom.

If you're a driver, you're used to driving on roads: observing speed limits, looking out for other drivers and pedestrians. You can go only where the roads go, and only in the direction they allow. You have to indicate, you have to stay in lane, and you have to be considerate of other road users. That's how business writing works.

Freewriting is less like driving in a town and more like riding a kite buggy in the middle of the world's biggest, emptiest desert; you can go any damn direction the wind takes you, as far and as fast as you like. There are no rules other than the imperative to raise your kite and allow the wind to power you: in this case, to create your prompt and then to write as fast and as honestly as you can until the timer goes off (and beyond, if you've caught a particularly good breeze).

And in case you still need convincing, the other great benefit of freewriting is that it's a great warm-up for any other kind of writing. It gets the words flowing without any pressure, and it helps you manage the fear of committing words to paper that can be so paralyzing. Once you know that you can write yourself out of any hole, indeed that writing is perhaps the best route out of a hole, you'll never be stumped by writer's block again.

One of my podcast guests, Orna Ross, taught me a useful mnemonic that captures the essence of freewriting: FREE = Fast, Raw, Exact and Easy.

Writing **fast** is the only way to keep up with your thoughts and to get them past the internal censor (who will leap in with 'You can't write THAT!' given a second's opportunity). It's **raw** partly because there's no need for the polish we usually put on writing – it doesn't matter if you don't use apostrophes or you misspell something – this is for you, not your English teacher.

And it's also **raw** because often you will find yourself writing things that feel uncomfortable, even painful, using language or revealing truths that you really wouldn't want to share with your English teacher, or anyone in fact. (And which you definitely wouldn't write in that lovely new notebook.)

It's **exact** because it challenges you not to use lazy generalizations, but to be precise about the details of your experience; to use your senses to really engage with and inhabit your writing.

And finally, it's **easy**: don't stress about it or over-complicate it; don't second-guess yourself or try to polish it up; don't worry if you're doing it right – you can't do this wrong. Just write, fast and raw, and see what happens.

You can just freewrite onto a blank page, and that's what Julia Cameron recommends: Morning Pages are a key practice in *The Artist's Way*, her 12-week course aimed at awakening creativity. But if you're using freewriting as a tool for business thinking rather than as a purely creative exercise, it can be more helpful to start with a prompt. I've suggested one over the page, but any question that's on your mind will do.

It doesn't matter how much you write and there's no word target: the only imperative is that you just keep writing, because if you stop and think you'll lose the flow. Writing by hand activates your brain more effectively than using a keyboard, and it doesn't give you the illusion that this is a finished, polished piece of work, or tempt you to edit as you go. It also means you can draw arrows, circle key points, even slip into drawing rather than writing (see Chapter 12 for more on this) – all of this is frictionless on paper, but not on screen.

A word of warning: for the first two or even three or four minutes you will almost certainly feel like this isn't working. That's completely normal. Just keep going. When you start working a rusted-up pump it's hard work and you get nothing but sludge at first. But if you keep pumping, suddenly, magically, the water starts to flow. It might take a few seconds or a few minutes, but if you keep writing, I promise you'll hit that moment where the mental sludge gives way to a sudden rush of clean, clear, sparkling water.

Ready? Enough theory already. Find yourself a big scruffy pad of paper and a pen or pencil, put yourself somewhere you won't be disturbed for six minutes (even if that's the bathroom). Write the following prompt at the top of a sheet of paper, then set a timer for six minutes and just write, as fast as you can, whatever comes into your head in response: *My greatest strength is...*

Once the timer's gone off, read back over your scribbles and notice the sensemaking that took place: perhaps you went back into the past to consider the roots of your strength, or told stories that illustrated how it works for you, or looked forward to ways that it might help you succeed in the future. What surprised you? What's helpful and what's not so helpful about what you discovered? What do you need to explore further? What might you do in response to those insights?

If you have the time (and your aching hand is up to it), you might want to do another writing sprint to explore one of those ideas.

Getting comfortable with freewriting is essential to developing an exploratory writing practice, and (as with anything in life) the more often you do it, the easier and more fluid it becomes.

Over the course of the next few chapters there'll be lots more opportunities to practise freewriting for different applications; we're going to start by turning our sensemaking spotlight away from ourselves and onto other people, especially the other people who drive us a bit crazy...

Empathy

Empathy is defined by the *Collins English Dictionary* as 'the ability to share another person's feelings and emotions as if they were your own'.[3] This isn't just about altruism and being better humans – Google's Project Oxygen and Project Aristotle discovered that empathy was one of the key indicators for its highest-performing employees and teams.[4]

But like anything worthwhile, empathy takes a bit of time and attention. We're so busy focusing on our own needs and experience that it doesn't always come naturally to factor in other people's – but if we do, the results can be extraordinary. This is a particularly powerful exercise to try with someone you don't feel instinctively warm towards, or alternatively you could try it with someone with whom you want to build a stronger relationship.

Empathy requires an imaginative leap, and the storytelling aspect of sensemaking lends itself beautifully to enabling this. By imagining someone else's experience and perspective in an exploratory writing session, we can make connections and see insights and possibilities that can transform our understanding of the other person. It's important to emphasize that the key question here is not whether we're right, necessarily, about the other person's feelings, motivations or experiences – we can never know that. (Let's face it, most of the time we're not really clear about our own feelings and motivations, never mind anyone else's.) The value of this exercise is that by allowing ourselves to consider things from their perspective we are able to 'see' them more richly and to relate to them more compassionately and thoughtfully; you'd be amazed at what that can achieve in a tricky relationship.

A useful prompt for an empathy exploration is a recent message from the person you have in mind, or even just a comment that's stuck in your mind for some reason. Perhaps you found it challenging or irritating in some way. Begin by rereading or remembering that message, and then start freewriting about what might lie behind it.

What needs might that person be seeking to meet? What fears and frustrations might they have? What might they be trying to achieve? What action or reaction might they be hoping for from you? Why does this matter to them? Remember that you can never know for sure, but draw on your curious explorer's mindset and keep the focus on them rather than you.

After you've written, take a moment to read back and reflect: does what you've considered today change your response to the original message, and if so in what way? What might it mean to use that empathetic experiment more habitually at home and at work?

One of the reasons that this is such a powerful exercise is that it subverts the 'attribution bias' – our tendency to attribute other people's negative behaviour to disposition, i.e. fixed character traits, rather than situation, while we often excuse our own shortcomings as situational. If for example we're abrupt with someone, we might excuse it by saying something like 'I was really busy and stressed that morning.' If someone's abrupt to us, however, we're more likely to think: 'Wow. What a rude person.' Deliberately engaging with someone else's perspective in this way, taking their part, means that we effectively apply this bias in their favour. It reminds us that there are multiple possible narratives in any encounter, which can help us let go of our more unhelpful interpretations. When you get into the habit of seeing those around you with more empathy, and become more willing to attribute their inexplicably irritating behaviours to situational factors rather than labelling them rude, selfish or stupid, it can transform your relationships.

Reframing

The exercise in empathy above is an example of reframing: changing the way you look at something in order to change your thoughts and feelings about it. Reframing is a fundamental technique in modern CBT (cognitive behaviour therapy) but its roots are older: as Marcus Aurelius put it, 'Reject your sense of injury and the injury itself disappears'.[5]

This is a key element of sensemaking in exploratory writing: deliberately exploring alternative interpretations of our experience. Sounds a bit too vague and mystical? Here's a very simple technique you can use to get started: counterfactuals.

Counterfactuals

The ability to imagine things that are counter to the facts is one of our superpowers as human beings. It's also a curse. When we think counterfactually, we imagine how things could have been if an event had turned out differently, or if we'd taken a different decision.

Counterfactual thinking is rarely neutral. (Where's the fun in that?)

Typically, we engage in one of two variations of counterfactual thinking: upwards or downwards.

Upward counterfactuals imagine how things could have been better. They typically involve the phrase 'if only'. Or, as John Greenleaf Whittier more poetically put it: 'For all sad words of tongue and pen, The saddest are these, "It might have been."'[6]

We use upward counterfactual thinking from the mundane – 'If only I'd brought an umbrella' – to the most profound griefs of our lives: 'If only he hadn't got on that plane.' Dan Pink examines this upwards counterfactual thinking in *The Power of Regret*, which reveals just how common it is: to regret, it seems, is human.

'If only…' can destroy us. We can never have that moment again; it's too late to do what we might have done. 'If only' almost always makes us *feel* worse. But, Pink points out, it can make us *do* better. This is what he means by the power of regret: the regrets that stay with us demonstrate what matters to us, and they may also help us make better choices next time – to speak up, to be bolder, to remember the umbrella.

The other kind of counterfactual thinking is downwards: 'at least'. 'At least it's not raining hard,' 'At least I got to tell him I love him.' We imagine how things could have been worse, and we take comfort from that. This kind of thinking makes us feel better, but it can also stop us engaging with the tough learnings.

Both varieties of counterfactuals can be useful in exploratory writing.

Let's experiment with upwards counterfactuals first: set a timer for just one minute and write as many sentences as you can, as quickly as you can, starting with the words 'If only…'. Don't stop to think, don't censor yourself, don't consider anything as being too trivial or too painful.

If you're like most of us, you'll end up with a mixed bag of regrets ranging from the laughable to the almost unbearable. These are your raw material for the two suggested exercises that follow: you of course are free to do either, both or neither, as you please.

Exercise 1

The If Only/At Least Flip. This is a quick thought experiment that supports mental resilience and can be used on the fly every day as necessary. It works best for low-level regrets, but can be used, with caution, for the bigger-ticket items too. Take one of your 'If only' statements and flip it to find a complementary downward counterfactual. For example:

'If only I'd checked that email before sending it…' / 'At least I didn't copy in the whole company…'

'If only I'd listened when they told me he was no good for me…' / 'At least I had the sense not to marry him…'

'If only I'd prepared the numbers better for the pitch…' / 'At least I won't make that mistake next time…'

At one level this is just a simple linguistic trick, but its contribution to resilience and wellbeing can be enormous. Yes, you may find some of these facile, you may even have had a strong impulse to punch anyone who'd tried to offer them as comfort, but they are just as 'true' and just as valid as any 'if only'. And you may discover not just comfort but strength there.

(NB: this works best when you do it for yourself. By all means encourage others to try their own counterfactual flips – though you might not want to use that terminology – but if you push 'at least' down others' throats while they're still in the grip of 'if only', you're unlikely to do much good and may do considerable harm.)

Exercise 2

The second exercise involves resisting the opportunity to make yourself *feel* better, and leaning into the regret to see if there's a way it can help you *do* better in the future. Choose one of the 'If only' statements you first wrote down. What can it teach you? What does it mean for you today? What could you do differently tomorrow in the light of it?

When I write honestly into an 'If only...', I often find that it is in fact an excuse: 'If only I had the time...', 'If only I could find the right person to help...'. These 'If only' statements are not really regrets; they are smokescreens. All too often, if I'm honest, I discover the real issue is something deeper: fear, or simply a failure to prioritize. And that I can do something about.

In a way, every aspect of exploratory writing is a form of sensemaking. But that would make for a very long chapter, and our next adventure deserves a chapter all of its own.

Chapter 7

Adventures in inquiry

*I*nquiry is simply the act of asking questions to which we don't know the answer – or even questions to which we think we *do* know the answer, but which we're open to reconsidering. It's how curiosity expresses itself, and as we saw in Chapter 3, curiosity is at the heart of exploration.

Much of the time though, as leaders and experts, or even as teachers, parents, partners and friends, we deal in answers. Other people ask questions of us, drawing on our expertise and experience. Our ability to give confident answers about our area of expertise lies at the root of our status and self-image.

Which means questions can be troublesome, particularly in the workplace.

While we remain in our area of competence, where we have more answers than questions, we're in our comfort zone and can work efficiently. When you've put in your 10,000 hours of practice at a skill to achieve mastery, you probably won't be delighted when some newbie comes along and asks why you're doing it like that.

And when we're talking about static skills, that makes sense. The apprentice probably should just shut up and watch the master craft a violin, rather than making suggestions on Day 1.

But most professional skills in the 21st century are not static. The pace of disruptive change is so fast that if we spend all our time cosied up with our answers, doing what we've always done, assuming what we've always assumed, one day we'll wake up to find that they and we have become gradually, irrevocably wrong. The solution? Get better at finding and asking questions, or if you prefer the fancy name, inquiry.

You used to be *great* at this. Between the ages of two and five, the average child asks around 40,000 questions[1] – increasingly demanding explanations rather than facts. (Before I had kids I promised myself I'd embrace the endless 'why' questions and I did try, but I'm not going to lie: it can get wearing.) As Alison Gopnik so eloquently puts it: 'Babies and young children are like the R&D division of the human species.'[2] There is literally nothing they will not question.

Once they get to school, however, the questions typically tail off. Most teachers prefer to be the ones asking the questions, and who can blame them? They have targets to hit and exams to prepare for. There's precious little space for curiosity in most classrooms because there's no time to go off-piste. This is changing, at least in more progressive schools. Inquiry-based learning – getting students to ask questions and discover the answers for themselves – is gaining popularity, mainly because it's proving a much more effective and engaging way of helping kids understand and retain the lesson. Older students, including those on professional courses, are usually encouraged to engage in reflection, responding to questions focused on how they handled a project and what they might do differently next time. This kind of reflection may also involve research: what's the latest thinking on this? How have others solved the problem? And what additional questions do those answers raise?

But somehow neither our natural childhood curiosity nor what we know about how to develop effective thinking and practice in the formal learning environment typically filter through into most offices. That doesn't mean you can't smuggle inquiry into your own workplace, for yourself and, perhaps more stealthily, for your colleagues. Warren Berger considers this an essential skill for 21st-century work, quoting entrepreneur Joi Ito:

> As we try to come to terms with a new reality that requires us to be lifelong learners (instead of just early-life learners), we must try to maintain or rekindle the curiosity, sense of wonder, inclination to try new things, and ability to adapt and absorb that served us so well in childhood. We must become neotenous (neotony being a biological term that describes the retention of childlike attributes in adulthood). To do so, we must rediscover the tool that kids use so well in those early years: the question.[3]

You may be familiar with inquiry as a tool for self-development in your professional life if you've worked with a coach: a good coach is less about providing answers and much more about asking great questions to help you understand an issue better and create your own solutions.

Sadly, you can't always have a coach in the room with you, but by mastering inquiry as part of an exploratory writing practice you can essentially become your own coach at any moment of the day or indeed, if it's a particularly chewy situation, night. As Helen Tupper and Sarah Ellis put it, becoming your own coach simply involves developing 'the skill of asking yourself questions to improve self-awareness and prompt positive action'.[4]

The most foundational part of inquiry is of course the question you ask. And not all questions are equal. You probably know already about closed and open questions: when I ask my son 'Did you have a good day?' when he comes back from school, I typically get a monosyllabic grunt by way of answer. Which is no more than I deserve – it's a lame question. When I remember to ask a more open, more interesting question – 'What's the coolest thing that happened today?' for example – I get a much more interesting response.

There are questions that are even less helpful: I remember with shame as a teenager shouting at my mother 'Why do you always spoil everything?' and of course there's no answer to that, just a whole lot of hurt. Most of us have learned not to speak to other people like that by the time we're out of our teens, but for some reason we still use that kind of talk to ourselves: 'What's wrong with me?' 'Why do I always mess up?'

As we saw in Chapter 2, one of the reasons that questions are so powerful is that when the brain is presented with a question – any question – the instinctive elaboration reflex kicks in and it immediately starts trying to come up with an answer. Instinctive elaboration can be a curse or a superpower: it all depends on the questions we ask ourselves. A toxic question like 'Why am I so useless?' will force your brain to busy itself finding some pretty unhelpful supporting evidence and ideas to try to answer it. But you can see the potential. As Tony Robbins puts it: 'Successful people ask better questions, and as a result, they get better answers.'[5]

So how can we use exploratory writing to help us ask better questions, of ourselves and of others, so that we get better, more useful answers?

Here are some ideas…

Town hall

One way to get started with this is with what I now call the 'town hall technique', after my Extraordinary Business Book Club conversation with Megan Hayes, author of *The Joy of Writing Things Down*. We have the idea, she said, that we're a single conscious entity (à la Descartes, 'I think therefore I am'), and that we have a unified response to an idea or situation, whereas actually there are often multiple reactions going on inside us at any point.

To put it another way: if you were asked to do a big presentation at work next week and you put the question to yourself: 'How do I feel about this?', your immediate answer might be 'Terrified!

This is awful! How do I get out of it!?' But if you were to look a little more carefully, become more conscious with your self-inquiry, you might discover there's much more going on. There may be a part of you that's excited by the idea, a part that's curious about what that experience would be like, even a part that's already quietly started planning how you might structure your ideas. We are what psychologists term 'a society of selves':

> Once we start getting into dialogue and practising that, we find there are many characters in there and our job is to be the integrating force, the CEO that draws all those voices into union, does a kind of town hall meeting if you like… And once you start engaging with those different voices, which I think writing really helps us to do, you find that you can get much more creative solutions.[6]

The big negative emotions tend to drown out the quieter, more curious or thoughtful voices, but by holding a more systematic self-inquiry, we can notice and explore those other perspectives.

When I run a town hall meeting for my own complicated, incoherent inner babble, I start by giving the stage to the noisiest voice – usually Fear. It's demanding to be heard, so there's no point trying to focus on anything else until it's had its say, and Fear doesn't usually need a prompt to get started. Often just letting it rant until it runs out of steam is enough to help me see how lame/unhelpful it is. But then comes the magic: then I invite the other stakeholders-in-me to take the stage. Fear shambles off, exhausted, and up comes my inner Researcher who has some ideas on how to move this forward, and I ask the question: 'What do YOU think?'

Try a town hall of your own. Think of a situation you're facing that you're anxious about, or that you feel is beyond you, and write a prompt such as 'town hall meeting to discuss X'. Let your instinctive reaction have its say first (what will you call it? Fear? Inner Critic? Something else?). And once it's had its say, invite some other, quieter voices to take the floor and ask: 'What do YOU think about this?' Here are some suggestions:

- Researcher
- Child
- Parent
- Teacher
- Manager
- Rebel
- Artist
- Explorer
- Future you (see p. 75)

You may come up with more in the course of your writing!

Simply discovering your own multiplicity is oddly liberating. As Walt Whitman so insouciantly put it: 'Do I contradict myself? Very well then I contradict myself (I am large, I contain multitudes).'[7]

No matter how many inner voices we discover, they are still all fundamentally aspects of ourselves. Which is as you'd expect, given that exploratory writing is essentially a solo sport. But that doesn't mean we can't involve others, even if they're not aware we're doing it; in fact, inquiring of others *in absentia* is a very helpful mental trick for lifting us out of a cognitive rut.

Inquiring of others

We live in a world where the contents of others' brains are available to us in myriad ways: through books, blogs, TED talks, articles, live video and more. Rather than just consuming such content, why not take an inquiry-based approach to turn that author or speaker into your personal coach without them even knowing?

This is a fun exercise. First select a resource you particularly like – for example, a book, video or article that you've found useful or thought-provoking recently. For a six-minute exploratory writing sprint you'll need to zoom in on a short section, but this is a technique you can use at a more leisurely, sustainable pace whenever you're engaging with quality content.

Begin by drawing a line down the middle of your sheet of paper and write the name of the author or speaker of the material you're using at the top of the left-hand column. And then, instead of setting your timer for six minutes as usual, I suggest that you set it just for three minutes initially. For those first three minutes, focus on the resource you've found, and as you read or listen, make a note of anything that seems significant to you in the first column. (Imagine you're a student, and you're going to have to write an essay on this later.)

When the timer goes off, you should have at least one or two notes in your left-hand column – so far, so standard. You've probably done this in a thousand lectures or conferences. But now we're going to apply some inquiry in that second column to transform this from simply consuming ideas to actively co-creating them.

You might already have some thoughts about what you want to do with the insights you've uncovered, in which case feel free to stop reading now and start an exploratory writing session of your own while the idea's fresh in your mind. But if you'd like a prompt, I suggest you write the simple but profound question 'What does this mean for me?' at the top of the second column. And for the next three minutes (or longer if you can), imagine that you are sitting alongside that speaker or writer and they are coaching you directly, one-to-one. How does the point they've just made apply to you? What advice would they give for the situation you're facing?

You can't know exactly what they'd say, of course, but simply by engaging imaginatively in that conversation and adopting their perspective, you shift from your own perspective and open yourself to new ideas. And that's when the magic happens.

Inquiring of future you

As well as using exploratory writing to enable the great and good to coach us without their knowledge, we can use it to access an even more powerful mentor: our future selves.

If you're a Harry Potter fan, you'll remember the scene where Harry travels in time and stands by the side of the lake watching his past self be attacked by Dementors. He's waiting for his father to appear and conjure the Patronus spell that he knows is about to save him and then it dawns on him: it wasn't his father he saw dimly across the lake as he was being attacked; it wasn't his father that saved him – it was he himself. He casts the spell, saves himself, and when Ron asks him how he managed it, he says: 'I knew I could do it… Because I'd already done it.'[8]

Which is mind-bending, in the way that time travel fiction always is, but also, again like the best fiction, rings true. Even if you're not a Potter fan, trust me when I say that future you has an extraordinary capacity to empower present-day you.

If present-day you is stuck on something, present-day you is unlikely to suddenly come up with the answer. Because if it was that easy, you wouldn't be stuck. But future you? Future you has solved this problem – all you need to do is ask how.

So yes, this is a mind trick, but it's an incredibly effective one. It also works in other ways too: you can ask future you about their – your – habits, relationships, day-to-day life, priorities, achievements and more.

This technique draws on key skills you've already mastered, including freewriting, empathy and inquiry, together with a new one, the powerful psychological tool of visualization to access truths that are imagined rather than real, but nonetheless useful for that.[9]

There are two keys to this exercise: the first is that you allow yourself to access the RIGHT future you, the one who has fulfilled your highest potential and purpose. If you're going to benefit from your own hindsight, you might as well pick the version of yourself with the most to teach.

The second is that you 'become' that future you for the duration of the exercise, rather than thinking of future you as an 'other'. So as you write, use the present tense to refer to the period you're visiting in the future, whether that's 1, 2, 5 or 20 years from now, and speak about your present-day challenge in the past tense, as something already overcome.

While you can do this exercise cold, it can be immensely helpful to close your eyes and listen to a guided visualization. You can access an audio version of the text below at www.exploratorywriting. com. Or simply read the following and then spend a few minutes visualizing the scene for yourself before you begin writing.

Begin by taking a deep, slow breath... and release it quietly and fully. Repeat as necessary until you feel your energy calming and slowing, and you feel ready to begin.

Now imagine that you find yourself in front of a house, a house that you've never seen before and yet somehow as soon as you see it you know that this is the place where your future self is completely happy. Take a moment to look at it: what do you notice? Where is it, and what's around you? What do you hear, feel, smell? Enjoy those sense impressions as you walk towards the door of the house and knock. After a few seconds, the door opens and you come face to face with your future self, smiling at you with recognition and love. You can't help but smile back, because it's wonderful to see yourself here, looking so at home. What do you notice about yourself? Your clothes? Your energy? The way you stand? You walk through the house together, and sit down beside a window. You know you can ask anything of your future self, and they'll answer honestly and with compassion and love. You could ask them how they overcame the problem that you're facing right now, or what were the key shifts they made in their life to bring them where they are today. As you look at them, what do you realize you most need from them right now? Allow the right question to form in your mind.

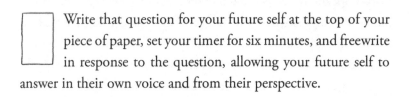

Write that question for your future self at the top of your piece of paper, set your timer for six minutes, and freewrite in response to the question, allowing your future self to answer in their own voice and from their perspective.

This is a more emotionally demanding task than many you have undertaken so far, so take a moment to notice your state once you've finished. How did it feel to meet future you? What struck you most forcibly about future you, and what does that mean for present-day you? What actions can you take today that will draw you closer to that image of your future self? Is there anything you need to stop doing to give you the space to become that person?

Remember too that future you is always available – whenever you feel under-resourced, you can access that fully resourced version of yourself and by using the power of inquiry, access their (your) strength and wisdom.

Finally, as well as uncovering more and more-useful answers, we can use inquiry-based exploratory writing to uncover more and more-interesting questions, too.

Question-storming

One fun and effective inquiry experiment is to flip the familiar idea of brainstorming: instead of trying to come up with as many ideas for answers/solutions as possible, challenge yourself to come up with as many questions related to the topic you're looking at as possible. Leadership and innovation expert Hal Gregerson stumbled across this technique accidentally while working with a sluggish group in a workshop, and developed it into a methodology he calls a 'question burst'. He suggests that this is primarily a group activity with a facilitator, and that is certainly an option, but as an exploratory writer this is also a technique you can use alone with just the blank page and a timer to provide the structure you need.

Focusing on questions rather than answers is surprisingly freeing: when you're ONLY allowed to come up with questions for which there is no obligation to suggest answers, the process feels playful and unpressured. As Gregerson puts it: 'Brainstorming for questions rather than answers makes it easier to push past cognitive biases and venture into uncharted territory.'[10]

Whereas inquiry-based exploratory writing typically begins with a question and goes on to explore possible answers, question-storming begins with a provocation statement as a springboard for question generation. My experience here is that it's not worth spending too much time and energy on the initial provocation: as long as it captures something that is a live issue for you, it will serve as a jumping-off point.

Here are some provocations I've used with myself and others in the past:

- 'This business is indistinguishable from its competitors.'
- 'We need to increase our revenue by 50% over the next year.'
- 'Our content marketing strategy is tired and ineffective.'

Just as with traditional brainstorming, one question leads to another, and no question is out of bounds.

Give it a go. Come up with a provocation for your own situation – or use one of those above if it feels useful. Set your timer for six minutes and come up with as many questions related to that provocation as you possibly can. Your questions might range from the profoundly philosophical ('What does success mean, anyway?') to the down-and-dirty tactical ('What software do I need for that?') and everything in between.

When the timer goes off, you can choose to take a break and then do another sprint if there's more in the bag, or review the questions you have and move on to the next stage: filtering and sifting.

This might involve narrowing or expanding some questions as necessary (e.g. 'What does success mean?' might usefully be narrowed to 'What are the key success factors here?', whereas 'What software do I need for that?' might require an additional more open question such as 'Are our systems still fit for purpose?'). And it will certainly involve prioritizing some questions over others, no matter how tough that feels.

Try identifying the three questions that feel the most significant, and then take those forward as prompts for a more traditional exploratory writing sprint to start coming up with answers.

While we've been focusing here on inquiry as a tool for exploratory writing, it's so much more than that. As you start to see the benefit of this agenda-free, curious questioning in your exploratory writing practice, I hope you'll also start to use it more in life and work.[11]

Because good questions help us think differently, inquiry is closely related to creativity, the topic of our next adventure.

Chapter 8

Adventures in playfulness

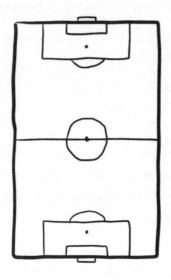

Remember that great word 'neotony' from the last chapter? It means 'the retention of childlike attributes in adulthood' (to save you looking back) and Joi Ito was using it specifically to refer to the importance of continuing to ask questions, which children do so freely, once we're grown up.

Another characteristic of children is their unselfconscious creativity. The same freshness and lack of experience that makes it easy to question things that more jaded adults take for granted also allows them to see things… differently.

When my son was quite small, I was delighted to hear that his primary school teacher had introduced them to philosophy. I asked him about the lesson.

'We were talking about apples.'

'Apples?'

'Yes. We had to rank them. You know, like an actual apple, then a photograph of an apple, then a drawing of an apple, then the word "apple", then an invisible apple...'

Impressive, I thought; they're introducing them to Plato's Forms. 'Why was the apple invisible?'

'Because I ate it.'

'Ah.'

This ability to take on board new ideas without blinking and run with them in unexpected directions is one of the most endearing characteristics of children, but it's also a vital skill in the 21st-century workplace, where new ideas and novel problems are coming at us all the time.

Just as with agency, intention and attention in Chapter 5, I believe there are three interconnected but distinct principles of playfulness at work, all of which lend themselves well to an exploratory writing approach: creativity, originality and problem solving.

Creativity involves finding a new approach to a situation (which might involve taking existing knowledge from one domain and applying it to another); originality is more about coming up with something qualitatively different from what already exists; and problem solving is simply about deploying both creativity and originality specifically in the service of... well, solving a problem.

Let's look at each in a little more detail and see how exploratory writing can help us develop these qualities.

Creativity

Even just 30 years ago, creative thinking was mostly reserved for a certain section of the population. The creative industries, we used to call them. And if you weren't in one of those – media, marketing, design, etc. – you could pretty much keep your creativity for your weekend art class and get on with the day job, thanks very much.

Today, creative thinking isn't a luxury for a chosen few: it's a key skill for everyone at every level of the organization. Which is a lot to ask of people who haven't necessarily thought of themselves as creative before and aren't sure how good they are at it. Exploratory writing comes into its own here, as it's a safe space in which to practise 'being creative'. It helps us develop our mental flexibility and playfulness, which builds our confidence in our ability to see a situation with fresh eyes and develop original ideas and solutions.

In one of the most-watched TED talks of all time, Sir Ken Robinson argued that creativity was just as important as literacy in education.[1] He claimed that schools and workplaces inhibit creativity by stigmatizing mistakes: if you're afraid to get something wrong, he reasoned, then you'll never come up with anything original. Exploratory writing in effect creates a space in which we are free to get things gloriously, creatively wrong without any penalty – a space otherwise unavailable to most of us in school or at work. And that significantly increases our chances of coming up with something interesting.

Creativity is very often based on connection – two ideas collide and they generate a spark that gives us a new perspective, insight or idea. As we saw in Chapter 2, we typically impose a bureaucratic model on the thinking we intend to communicate for public consumption, in which ideas are neatly organized and compartmentalized for ease of use and retrieval. This approach reduces the likelihood of these creative collisions. Inside our chaotic, swirling, freely associating brains, however, the magic is just waiting to happen: all we need is a pen moving fast enough and space enough on the page to capture those seemingly random associations so that we can figure out what – if anything – to do with them.

If you're like me, the minute someone says 'Be creative!' your mind shuts down in panic. So for this exercise we're going to come at things sideways and back to front, and focus on freeing ourselves up to get things gloriously, creatively wrong. Take a challenge at work or home that's on your mind right now, and instead of trying to come up with creative ideas for how to go about meeting it, give yourself six minutes of freewriting to come up with the most hilariously awful ideas you can for making it a complete failure. If you've been asked to come up with an idea for a new marketing campaign, for example, what images and catchphrases would have potential customers running for the hills? Have fun with this; be as outrageous as you like and enjoy the anarchic playfulness of messing up without any inhibitions.

Once you've finished, take a look at what you came up with. Most of it will be hopeless nonsense, of course, and that's totally fine.

But spend a few moments thinking what the opposite of these terrible ideas might be: you may find that by coming at things backwards, you've happened upon an interesting idea that's worth developing further.

(And if not, at least you'll have had fun trying.)

Originality

It's ironic that in an age where creativity and originality are talked about more than ever before, the opportunity to 'take inspiration from' (aka 'copy') others is off the scale.

Let's imagine it's your job to create a landing page for a new product. What's your first instinct?

If you're like the vast majority of us, you'll start by Googling. Are there any ideas out there you could 'borrow'? What have other people done that's similar? Is there a Canva template? After all, there's no point reinventing the wheel, right?

But if we always start something new by looking around to see what's already there, we're taking on board someone else's priorities, style, constraints and assumptions, not our own.

When you reach for someone else's work as a starting point for your own, it effectively limits the scope of your thinking. All bargain hunters know about the cognitive bias known as 'anchoring': go in with a ridiculously low price·and no matter how much the seller may protest, that's now the baseline for the negotiation. The reference point has been set, and it shapes the rest of the haggling.

Much the same thing happens when you base your own thinking on another person's ideas. You may change and adapt things to suit your own purposes, but the final result will be very different than it would have been if you'd started from scratch.

('It certainly will', you might say, 'It'll be a damn sight quicker and probably better'.)

Luckily, with exploratory writing it's possible to get the best of both worlds.

Think about something you need to produce that you'd usually look up online: a presentation, a report, a job description, a meal plan. Instead of reaching for the search box, pause a second. Grab a notepad and pen instead, and spend six minutes or so freewriting about what it is you want to achieve. Who is this for and what do they need? What's the most important outcome? How can you bring your unique mix of skill, experience and interest to this?

Once you've finished that exploratory writing sprint, if you still need to, feel free to start Googling. You'll be much better placed to recognize a good starting point when you find it, and you'll do a better job of adapting it to make it fit for YOUR purpose.

Problem solving

One reason why being creative and original are such great life skills is that they are key tools for problem solving. The very fact that something is a problem implies that your old or instinctive approach isn't working, and you need to try something new. Sensemaking and reframing (Chapter 6) and inquiry (Chapter 7) are all useful tools for tackling problems, but there are other more specific approaches, and you won't be surprised to hear that exploratory writing can be used to support these too.

First, a disclaimer: problem solving, especially at work, and especially for big problems, is big business. There are many different theories and multi-step methodologies, and a six-minute exploratory writing sprint clearly isn't intended to replace those. But just as most holes don't require a JCB to dig them, most problems don't demand a full-on methodology with supporting software.

That said, it's worth keeping the broad principles of these theories in mind. I used to teach on a business school MBA residential course on creativity, innovation and change (it was huge fun; how often do you get paid to help executives discover finger painting?), and it centred around a structured approach to creative problem solving that went something like this:

1. Articulate the problem: expand it to fully understand it, and make sure it really IS the problem you need to be fixing (problem exploration phase: it's amazing how often the presenting problem turns out to be a symptom, or even not a problem at all).
2. Generate lots of possible solutions (creative thinking phase).
3. Evaluate the options to identify the one(s) you're going to take forward (critical thinking phase).
4. Implement it (action phase).

If you don't keep the broad shape of that process in mind, it's all too easy to default to something much simpler and narrower:

1. Think of a possible solution.
2. Implement it.

That might work, sure, but the odds aren't great.

Try it out. Think of a relatively straightforward problem you're trying to solve at the moment (nothing too intractable or philosophical – this is everyday magic, remember, and we're still learning at this point) and focus not on possible solutions, but on exploring the problem itself.

'Why?' is a useful tool to use here: you can go upstream to seek out underlying causes ('Why is this happening?') or downstream to focus on consequences ('Why is this a problem?'), or mix up the two if you prefer. And as you come up with each underlying cause or consequence, ask 'Why?' again, and see what happens. (You may be familiar with this technique: in business circles it's known as the Five Whys, but you're equally likely to have encountered it in conversation with a preschooler.)

By going upstream to focus on underlying causes, you may discover that the REAL problem isn't necessarily the one you thought you had to solve; going downstream to consequences helps you find ways to mitigate or eliminate those. You might even realize that what you thought was a problem isn't really a problem at all; it's just something that's irritating you. And the best way to fix that is usually simply to decide not to let it irritate you anymore.

These three incredibly useful aspects of playfulness – creativity, originality and problem solving – can all benefit from one powerful tool that's an essential addition to your exploratory writing kit: the metaphor.

And that's what we'll explore in our next adventure...

Chapter 9
Adventures in transformation

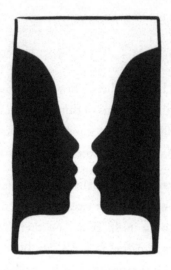

A s part of sensemaking, we can't help but reach for metaphor (there, I just did it myself, and I'm not even sorry). 'Metaphor' is simply the catch-all term for thinking about one thing in terms of another. There are other terms you might be familiar with that operate in this space too. Similes, such as 'Life is like a box of chocolates,' are a particular type of metaphor – they explicitly state that there's a similarity, rather than saying 'Life IS a box of chocolates.' An analogy is a metaphor that's being used for a purpose: to explain something in terms of something else (we'll look at analogy in more detail in Chapter 13). But most of our metaphors aren't so self-aware. They're buried so deep in our language and our thinking that most of the time we don't even see them, despite it being almost impossible to construct a sentence without them (there I go again: I just used two digging/building metaphors and a visual one, and I wasn't even trying).

Our reliance on metaphors means that they can be a powerful tool for mental magic if we learn how to make them work for us rather than against us.

Managing metaphors

We use metaphors because they're how our brains work – we find it much easier to think in terms of things we know and experience. We can access what we don't know and express what we can't express in terms of what we *do* know and what we *can* express.

That's a massive cognitive benefit. But there's a cognitive cost attached to metaphors too: it's easy to forget that the metaphor isn't actually the thing itself. If we use them intentionally, they can help us be more creative and solve problems, not to mention communicate our ideas more effectively to others. But if we're not aware of them, they can trip us up. Here are three ways metaphors can work against us:

1. They can generate unhelpful emotions
I'll never forget talking to a woman who was nearly in tears about her situation at work. She told me how she felt she was 'spinning plates', and I could hear in her voice the panicky fear that one day – and soon – one of those plates would fall and smash. No wonder she was stressed. And what a pointless way to spend your day! I invited her to consider whether there were any other metaphors

she could use to reflect the way her job involved so many different and competing priorities. We experimented with the idea of her work as a tapestry, drawing in different threads at different times to create the full picture, and it was remarkable to see how this new image transformed her emotional state. This metaphor was calmer, more creative and more purposeful, and she relaxed visibly as she developed it.

2. They can create conflict

If your idea of being part of an organization is based on a family metaphor, where people look out for each other and the key values are trust, acceptance and belonging, you'll soon find yourself in conflict with someone whose metaphor-in-use is an elite sports team, where you're only as good as your last result. Not until each person has understood the metaphor that underlies the other person's thinking can such conflicts be surfaced and resolved.

3. They can limit our ability to find solutions

A famous 2011 study by Paul Thibodeau and Lera Boroditsky showed how metaphors can constrain people's thinking about a problem without them realizing it.[1] They ran an experiment in which they talked about urban crime using one of two framing metaphors in each of the research subject groups: to one group they described crime as a disease infecting the city, and to the second they framed it as a beast preying on the city. And then they invited each group to suggest solutions. What they discovered was that even though the subjects weren't aware at a conscious level of the metaphor they'd been given, their solutions reflected that framing. Those in the group where crime had been discussed in terms of a virus took a diagnose/treat/inoculate approach, whereas those exposed to the idea of the preying animal used a capture/enforce/punish logic.

Exploratory writing can help us become more conscious and more curious in exploring the metaphors that we use every day, and to use metaphor more intentionally so that it serves us better.

But before we can start to work effectively with metaphors in exploratory writing, we first have to become aware of them.

Surfacing metaphors

This is a useful exercise to get your metaphor radar switched on (ooh, there's another one!) so that you can start to see how they might be influencing your attitudes and behaviour without you even realizing it.

The best way to start this exercise is to look back at a recent exploratory writing sprint, particularly one that was focused on sensemaking in a difficult situation. If you've already binned/shredded/incinerated all your past sprints, set the timer for six minutes and freewrite in response to this prompt: *My work is...*

Now look back over what you've written and have a go at picking out all the metaphors you've used. Remember they can be hiding in plain view – be ruthless in identifying anything that is not literally true; there'll probably be more than you imagine. What do you notice? Is there a dominant metaphor? Which ones strike you as most interesting? Are they helpful or unhelpful? How might they be limiting your thinking or framing your behaviour? Where might they have come from?

To get you started, here's an example of the kind of thing that often comes up:

My work is all-consuming. There's no time to sit and think about what I want to do; I'm just reacting constantly, firefighting. Whenever someone comes over to my desk I brace myself because I know they're going to throw something else at me and I'm going to have to keep that in the air too. It's just exhausting, and my colleagues don't seem to appreciate what I'm dealing with; they keep adding fuel to the fire. My boss is even worse – not only does he not realize how hard I'm running just to stay still, he keeps preaching about 'big picture thinking' and 'personal development' – which is fine for him, sitting in the captain's quarters while we sweat in the engine room – who's got time for that down here where the real work is happening?

There are so many metaphors here that communicate a panicky, overwhelmed state of mind: all-consuming (suggesting a ravenous monster); trying to put out fires while others fuel them; having things thrown at you; running without moving forwards; imagining the boss as both a preacher in the pulpit and the captain in his plush quarters; sweating in a claustrophobic engine room…

How are those mental images shaping the writer's emotional state, do you think? What is the likely impact on their work, and on their relationships with their boss and colleagues?

Granted, this is something of a metaphor riot, but it's not a million miles from some of the responses people have shared with me in workshops. And what's interesting is that most of those people had no idea that they were using those metaphors in the first place, and were shocked to realize the impact they might be having on their reactions, emotions, relationships and behaviour at work.

Once you're aware of the metaphors you're using unconsciously, you can consciously choose to change them. Just as the woman who had seen herself spinning plates decided to think instead in terms of creating a tapestry from the different threads of her responsibilities, you might decide that instead of seeing your boss swanning around the captain's quarters while you sweat below, it would be more constructive to see them as the cox in the boat you're rowing with your colleagues, keeping an eye on direction and coordinating your efforts. Will it change their behaviour? Not directly, but it will change your attitude, which changes *your* behaviour, and that is what ultimately changes others' behaviour towards you.

Once you've done this exercise for yourself, you'll notice that you become more tuned in to metaphors generally (there's another one, look) and better able to spot them in other people's language as well as your own. Which means you're better equipped to understand how those ways of seeing the world are shaping their experience and attitudes. Next time you're talking to someone about something challenging, or you receive a difficult email, get forensic: look for the metaphors in use and think about how they might be influencing their feelings about that situation. (You could use this as a variation on the empathy exercise back in Chapter 6.)

Surfacing metaphors in use is one thing: finding new, more helpful ones is another skill altogether. One of my favourite ways to do this – part useful cognitive exercise, part party trick – is the forced metaphor.

Forced metaphors

This is quite simply one of the most powerful, energizing, magical creativity techniques I know and once you have this in your back pocket you will *never* be stuck for something to write, or for solutions to problems. It builds on the sensemaking impulse of our brains, which just can't help creating patterns and finding connections in the most unpromising places.

The difference in this case is that there's no obvious story for our brain to create; it has to work hard, to make a creative cognitive leap to find connections that aren't apparent, so the sensemaking becomes a fully conscious process.

If you and I were sitting together and able to do this exercise in person – wouldn't that be great? – I'd simply ask you to take a walk outside and bring me back three things. They could literally be three things you bring back into the room with you or they might just be something you see that you come back to tell me about. So you might bring me an acorn, an empty crisp packet and a plane going overhead, for example. (I realize this is not exactly the stuff of Shelley and Keats, but bear with me.)

If you have the time and inclination, then by all means do that right now – take yourself off for a walk and bring back three things, either literally to put on your desk in front of you, or as an idea that you can write or draw on a post-it if it's something unsuitable for bringing indoors. If you can get outside, do: you'll find your energy and your creativity benefit simply from fresh air and nature! But if you can't get outside right now, then just look around the space you're in and identify three objects that catch your eye.

Got your three things? Good.

In this exercise, we're going to explore how these objects shed metaphorical light on an issue you're facing. So that's the final step: select a live problem or situation that you'd like a fresh perspective on. It could be a tricky relationship, a resourcing or structural issue, anything.

And yes, I realize that you're probably looking at your objects and thinking – really? But this is exactly the point: there's no obvious point of similarity here so you're really going to have to work to find connections. When you find them, you're going to feel surprised and delighted, and they're going to show you something you've never seen before – and that, my friend, is the power of metaphor.

Brian Eno put it beautifully: 'If you want to end up somewhere different it is a good idea to start somewhere different.'[2] What we're doing here is giving you somewhere completely different to start, and that does something magical to your brain.

People doing this exercise for the first time often worry about it: they can't see how it will work, and they don't want to 'fail'. But remember, its power is not in how 'good' the objects that you've found are, or even how creative you are, but simply in the way your brain works. We've already encountered instinctive elaboration, that mental reflex that can't help but generate answers to any question, and the way that we're programmed to create meaning and make connections through sensemaking. It's those two fundamental neurological impulses that you're relying on here, not your own cleverness. The speed of a freewriting sprint means you can't overthink this: it allows you to get out of your own way and let your brain get on with the job.

So set your timer and take a good look at your three random items: your prompt for this sprint is simply 'X is like Y because…' where X is a problem or issue that's on your mind and Y is one of the objects you've found. If you strike gold with your first object, feel free to keep writing about that for the full six minutes; if you're struggling, try each item in turn until you get a toehold that will get you started – just use your judgement and write for as long as it's useful on each object and then turn to the next when the time is right.

Remember, nobody's judging how 'well' you performed on this task. And if it didn't work at all, hey, you only lost six minutes of your day. But I'm pretty confident that you will have surprised yourself with at least one or two insights from what seemed like such an unpromising premise.

When I was writing this section, I dutifully did this exercise again for myself. Having just returned from a run by the canal, I used 'travelling by narrow boat' as one of my prompts, and the issue I had at hand was recruiting a new hire. Even I, practised as I am with this technique, wondered at first if I'd chosen badly. For the first minute or so I just couldn't see a connection and my writing was getting a little desperate. Then suddenly I found myself writing:

> OK, there's something about having to have a place for everything, because there's no room to be disorganized, which is a bit like having to write everything down and systematize it because it's not just in my head any more...

And then:

> When you're travelling by narrow boat you've got to be really thoughtful about who you travel with because they've got to be handy with a rope and useful in a lock but also you've got to be able to get along together in an enclosed space so their attitude is really important – how can I incorporate that in a job description?

Both of those insights were relevant and helpful. It always comes good – just be open and playful and trust the process!

I'd encourage you to try this trick – and it does feel like a trick – several times, partly because it will help you come up with creative solutions to the problem at hand, of course, but also because it will build your confidence in your own ability to think out of the box whenever required. You don't need to sit around waiting for the right metaphor to arrive fully formed. Instead, you can start where you are and use whatever's to hand to enable you to kickstart your creativity. Knowing that you can essentially conjure up something from nothing at a moment's notice is a huge confidence boost.

So far, we've been looking at how exploratory writing can help us *be* better and *do* better, in life and work. For the final two chapters in this section we're going to look at how we can use it to help us *feel* better: to support our wellbeing.

Chapter 10
Adventures in self-knowledge

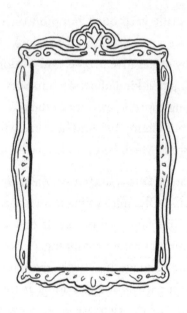

*B*ack in Chapter 2 we met the Chimp, the ancient, reactive (often over-reactive) part of our brain.

While taming the Chimp is a tricky business, exploratory writing can help in the lifelong task of learning to manage it more effectively.

I'm going to suggest three specific ways in which it can do so:

- by allowing the Chimp to feel that it's been heard;
- by acknowledging and celebrating the things that matter to the Chimp;
- by flipping the Chimp's instinctive negativity to generate more positive outcomes.

Hearing the Chimp

One reason we usually keep our Chimp on such a tight leash is because, frankly, we know it's not a good look. We don't much enjoy the company of negative people, and we don't want to get a reputation for being that kind of person ourselves. Another reason is that we fear losing control: once out of the box, we wonder, just how crazy might our Chimp be? And how bad will it make us feel to confront that stuff? Much better to keep a lid on it.

When Professor Steve Peters, author of *The Chimp Paradox*, was working with the GB Olympic cycling team he had a rule: athletes could come and complain to him, but if they did, they had to complain for 15 minutes without stopping. Nobody ever managed it.[1] It turns out that when we do actually give our Chimp free rein, it can't sustain its negativity for very long. It runs out of steam. But of course most of the time we *don't* allow the Chimp this full, free hearing, and so instead it provides a constant low-level grumbling drip feed of negativity, which we spend much of our time actively trying to ignore.

The Chimp wants to be heard, and not listening won't make it stop trying. Exploratory writing provides a safe, contained space in which to experiment with listening to what it has to say – to notice the truth within it and also the things that may not be true, which we can then go on to consider rationally and answer with evidence as appropriate.

In this writing session, your Chimp gets its day. Think about a situation that's causing you some negative emotion – it could be a conflict, a frustration with yourself or others, or something you're angry or ashamed about. (Be sensible here – this is everyday magic for everyday frustrations, so choose something manageable, not real trauma where support from a professional therapist would be more appropriate.)

And then for six minutes, give your Chimp free rein with the freewriting. Let it say exactly what's on its mind, how it feels, why it feels like this, and just how unfair it all is. Have a good old pity party or rant onto the page. Don't judge; just notice what you notice. You probably won't need a prompt, but if you want one, try this: ***I can't tell anyone this but...***

It can be quite moving or unsettling to hear what your Chimp has to say, so as you read back over what you've written, be kind to yourself. It may help to imagine yourself as a counsellor or simply a good friend listening to someone in pain: we're generally much kinder to others than we are to ourselves.

Typically in this exercise, people notice that there are elements of truth and elements of not-truth: exaggeration, catastrophizing, generalization, supposition and so on. Often the truth relates to our most fundamental needs, for example for recognition, safety, freedom and so on. Learning to identify our own 'fingerprint needs' (as Alice Sheldon calls them[2]) can help us understand not only why our Chimp might be triggered, but also how to ensure that we find solutions that meet those needs rather than denying them. With practice, we will also become more skilled at noticing such needs in others, which is where practising empathy for ourselves expands so helpfully to make it easier for us to empathize with others.

Celebrating the Chimp

Once you've heard what your Chimp has to say, your Human has to decide what to do with that new understanding.

You're probably already aware that simply writing down negative thoughts reduces their power – this is called 'affect labelling' and it's a well-established technique for emotion regulation. We're going to go a step beyond that today and not just mitigate the negative impact of the Chimp but seek out something to celebrate within it.

Crazy, right? What could there possibly be to celebrate in all that negativity? But remember that the things that create the strongest emotions in us are those things that matter most to us. As Alice Sheldon puts it:

> If we can start to understand that our feelings are valuable messengers about our needs, we can accept them, make sense of what they're telling us, and act on them with awareness. Rightly understood, our feelings are a resource rather than a distraction that gets in the way. They're an indicator of what's important to us in any given moment.[3]

To put it another way, if you can spot the things that most agitate your Chimp, you can discover what most matters to you. Dan Pink makes a similar point when talking about regrets:

If we understand what people regret the most, we understand what they value the most... So when people tell you their regrets, they're actually telling you indirectly what they value.[4]

Another reason to celebrate your Chimp is that it's proof your instincts are working properly: it's powered by fear, and if it weren't for fear, you wouldn't have survived long enough to be reading this book. Elizabeth Gilbert talks beautifully about the way she changed her relationship with fear to recognize it as an inevitable part of the creative process, rather than trying to overcome it or shout it down:

I speak to it very lovingly. I have a lot of compassion for it as an entity. Over time, I've realized that this isn't a glitch in me. This is a built-in; this came right out of the factory. Fear has an evolutionary mission, which is, "Do not do something new, or that we don't know the outcome of—because it could end in death." Fear is always going to be present when you try to do anything creative because creativity asks you to try something new, and you don't know what the outcome will be... I used to fight it. I used to think I needed to be braver, and I don't think I need to be braver. I think I need to be kinder and I need to be more curious. And bravery comes from that.[5]

Your Chimp may say hurtful things, but once you realize that at the root of it all is this relentless drive to keep you safe, it's easier to respond to that with compassion and to choose to act anyway. You can acknowledge the potential pain your Chimp sees and accept it as a price worth paying for the potential gain that you see.

So for this exercise, you're going to spend six minutes writing a thank you letter to your Chimp, appreciating it rather than trying to squash it back into its box or shout it down. Look back at the writing you did for the exercise above with fresh, more compassionate eyes: what do you notice that's helpful? Where does your Chimp's uncensored honesty reveal things that you hadn't realized were so important to you? How is it trying to keep you safe?

You may still feel that you're not quite able to celebrate your Chimp, but at least you understand it a little better now. And if your Chimp feels appreciated, it's likely to be less troublesome in the future. (This goes for most humans, too.)

Flipping the Chimp

Another ninja way to respond to this outpouring of negativity is not just to engage with the Chimp but to flip it. Having articulated some of those negative stories and beliefs, and brought them out into the light where you could look at them in the first exercise, in this exercise you'll write through them and out the other side to the point where you will be able to recognize them as potential superpowers.

Now, I don't know what your Chimp threw at you in the first writing session of this section. But whatever it is, you now have a number of stories that your Chimp is telling you about yourself and your life, and the chances are they're pretty crude and cruel. Here are some examples that often come up when I run this exercise in workshops:

'I have nothing original to say.'
'I'm disorganized and lazy.'
'I'm no good with money.'
'I always say the wrong thing.'
'Nobody likes me.'

These are tough to hear and, on the surface of things, pretty unhelpful. But you already know that whatever cruel, negative things your Chimp is saying to you, deep down it is simply trying to keep you safe. It's terrified of risk and the fear of failure or abandonment. So if we're going to change the story here, we're going to have to be smarter than just lamely shouting back: 'That's not true!' Instead, we're going to use an exploratory writing form of ju-jitsu and use the power of that negativity against itself to generate something more helpful.

On as big a sheet of paper as you can find, draw a line so you have two columns: a narrow one on the left and a much wider one on the right. At the top of the left-hand column write 'What the Chimp said' and at the top of the right-hand column write 'How I flipped the Chimp'.

And here's where the magic happens: you're going to flip each negative statement that came up in the previous writing session into a superpower. As before, it helps to pretend you're talking about someone else, perhaps an insecure friend, to give you a bit of distance and compassion.

So for example, if your Chimp told you that you don't have enough experience for the challenge or role in front of you, you could flip that into a superpower by recognizing that your lack of experience means you are more humble, open minded and motivated to learn than someone with more experience in the role.

Think of yourself as a prosecuting lawyer determined to make the case against the Chimp, if that helps, and have fun with this. What you're doing is further challenging the Chimp's narrative, showing yourself alternative narratives, and also practising playfulness and resilience.

So get your timer ready, prepare those two columns – 'What the Chimp said' and 'How I flipped the Chimp' – freewrite in response, and see what happens!

It can be tricky getting the balance between allowing your Chimp's deep-seated negative stories to come out into the open and meeting them with the more positive responses of recognition, compassion and curiosity. If you don't feel you've got it quite right yet, don't worry: this is a lifelong practice, not a one-time performance.

But as you use exploratory writing more regularly, you'll start to trust the page more as a safe space to surface the negative emotions without judgement – the fears, regrets, frustrations, and even the insults – and you'll gain confidence in your ability to look at them with compassion and curiosity. They're just stories you're telling yourself, and they reveal useful things about you: but you have the power to take and use what's helpful, rewrite what's not and move on with your life.

Getting to know ourselves more fully and accept the aspects of ourselves that we find difficult is one way in which exploratory writing can help us feel better (as opposed to simply do better). But it's not the only way – let's think more broadly in the next chapter about wellbeing.

Chapter 11

Adventures in wellbeing

What IS wellbeing, anyway? I know it when I see it – or rather, when I feel it – but when I first came to write this chapter I realized I didn't know exactly how to define it.

Of all the definitions I researched, the one that made the most sense to me was by a group of researchers from Cardiff Metropolitan University in 2021. They define wellbeing as: 'the balance point between an individual's resource pool and the challenges faced…

Stable wellbeing is when individuals have the psychological, social and physical resources they need to meet a particular psychological, social and/or physical challenge.'[1]

I like this definition for several reasons. First because it allows for infinite individual flexibility: I might think of speaking in front of 100 people as a challenge; you might do that without blinking before breakfast. That flexibility doesn't just apply between different individuals, of course, but for the same individual at different times on the same day, depending on the dynamic tension between resources and challenges in the moment. I go out for a run every day without a second thought, but one night when I returned home late from a trade fair, frazzled and exhausted with aching feet, I found myself nearly in tears as I laced up my trainers so as not to break my streak: the prospect of running a couple of laps of the park felt so unmanageable I might as well have been setting out on the Marathon des Sables. My depleted physical resources were unequal to what would on any other day have been no challenge at all.

The second reason I like this definition is that it implies that not having challenges is just as unhealthy as being overwhelmed – just as psychologist Mihaly Csikszentmihalyi showed that happiness, or in his words 'the flow state', is to be found in a relatively narrow band bounded by anxiety on the one hand and boredom on the other.[2]

And the final reason I like this definition, and the one that's most relevant in the context of exploratory writing, is that it reveals that we need not necessarily be overwhelmed by any challenge *if* we can balance it, sooner or later, by increasing our resources.

Resourcing ourselves

How do we increase our resources? The Cardiff researchers identify three types of challenge and resources: psychological, social and physical (or a mix of these). I'm going to work backwards through these, contrariwise, to assess where, if at all, exploratory writing might play a part.

Physical

There's no mystery here, really. We resource ourselves best physically with the ancient, non-negotiable principles captured neatly by coach Sara Milne Rowe as the SHED method: sleep, hydration, exercise, diet.[3] If you're hoping to hear that exploratory writing can replace any one of these, I'm sorry to disappoint you. But perhaps surprisingly it's not a complete loss on the physical front: there's evidence that exploratory writing can boost your immune system and help you sleep better,[4] so don't be too quick to write it off completely.

Social

Meaningful, positive relationships feature high on any psychologist's list of Things That Support Wellbeing and, again, you might think that exploratory writing has only a limited application here. You need to spend time with the people doing the things, right? But again, the solitary practice of exploratory writing turns out to have unexpected benefits in the social realm. It can help us work through relationship glitches in a safe space before we decide whether or not to have the stand-up row, for example. And by consciously exploring situations from other people's perspective we increase our empathy, which in turn benefits our relationships.

Sometimes it's not us, it's them, and perspective taking can help us understand why someone might be being such an irritating idiot, and how we might best approach the topic with them.

More of the time, though, and it pains me to admit it, it's not them, it's me. And when this is the case, self-knowledge exploratory writing tools such as those in the previous chapter can help me uncover the buttons that are being pressed and acknowledge my own irritating idiocy to myself, and explain it to others if necessary. At which point I'm better resourced to do something about it, which can only be good for the relationship. (Or alternatively it can reveal that the relationship has run its course – and that too can be a great result for wellbeing.)

Psychological

But it's in the last category, psychological challenges such as anxiety, negative self-talk or dissatisfaction (hello, Chimp!), that exploratory writing really comes into its own as a tool to help us resource ourselves and maintain our wellbeing.

At work we typically face uncertainty and overwhelm on a daily basis, often working remotely, always 'on'. When we go home (and post-pandemic, what I mean by 'go home' is simply 'stop what we usually think of as work and turn our attention to other aspects of life'), it doesn't necessarily get any easier. Whether you're listening to the news, juggling the household budget to accommodate soaring energy bills or planning to impress the neighbours at a dinner party, there's no shortage of stress. Some we choose; some is thrust upon us. (Note that I'm not speaking here about clinical depression or real trauma, which are best dealt with by the support of a trained professional, but about everyday anxieties, for which the everyday magic of exploratory writing is best suited.)

It's on this area of resourcing ourselves that we'll focus for the rest of this chapter, beginning with a brief look at the history of how writing has been proven to support our psychological health.

Therapeutic writing

We've understood for centuries that writing can have a therapeutic dimension. Responding to Plato's attack on poetry, Aristotle claimed that tragedy was valuable because it produced 'catharsis', the purging of the negative emotions of pity and fear, though to be fair he was talking about the effect on the audience rather than the tragedian. Freud too held that inhibiting emotions and trauma was dangerous, although he focused more on talking therapy than writing.

But it was in 1986 that the concept of expressive writing as a therapeutic tool gained prominence, following a seminal study by Pennebaker and Beall.[5] James Pennebaker had been studying the body's response to stress, specifically in relation to polygraphs, or lie detectors, and he noticed that after confessing their guilt, subjects appeared not just less stressed but positively relieved. He started to research the health implications of opening up about trauma rather than holding it in. To avoid the ethical and practical issues of asking people to open up and talk about deeply personal issues to strangers, he stumbled upon what he called 'expressive writing' as a more workable process.

The results were remarkable. The group encouraged to write for 15 minutes each day about past traumatic experiences showed significant long-term health benefits, including fewer visits to the doctor, and this finding was repeated in subsequent experiments. Those who engaged in expressive writing showed reduced anxiety, improved memory and sleep, and better performance at work compared to control groups.

Intrigued, Pennebaker did further studies to see if he could work out what it was about the writing practice that caused the most dramatic improvements. He discovered that the subjects reporting the most significant benefits tended to shift perspective over time, and also to use more 'sensemaking' words – 'realize', 'because', 'reason'. It wasn't simply catharsis that was making these people feel better, it was the processing of experience.

Julia Cameron talks about this in *The Right to Write*, too. She quotes an 'executive' who uses a powerful metaphor for exploratory writing as part of the work day:

> 'I just have so much to metabolise,' Joseph phrases it. 'In any given day I meet so many people and do so many things that I need a place to ask myself what I really think about all of it. Without writing, my life rushes by unexamined.'[6]

This isn't someone processing trauma, as with Pennebaker's subjects. Joseph, like you, like me, just has a load of stuff going on, and writing is the low-level, open-all-hours therapeutic intervention that keeps it from overwhelming him.

So with that impressive tradition and evidence base behind us, how do we apply exploratory writing to the nuts and bolts of wellbeing on a daily basis, at home and at work? I believe there are four key areas in which exploratory writing can support our psychological wellbeing:

- mental resilience;
- sensemaking for wellbeing;
- self-coaching;
- mindfulness.

Let's explore each of these further, reminding ourselves of some of the techniques and exercises we've already learned and trying out some new ones along the way.

Mental resilience

First, a reminder: therapeutic writing is beyond the scope of this book. So by 'mental resilience' here I mean everyday resilience: the ability to quickly regain a positive mental state and perform effectively after a disruptive or stressful event, which usually involves a degree of adaptation and flexibility.

Second, a disclaimer: the term 'resilience' is sometimes hijacked to deflect blame from a dysfunctional system that's causing stress for the individuals having to cope with it. In such cases, as Bruce Daisley points out, 'a call from others to be resilient is less than helpful'.[7] Fixing the system would be a massively better solution. But if fixing the system isn't in your gift, it makes sense to focus on what you *can* control, and that's your response to the stress, i.e. your resilience. I'm not saying this is right; I'm just being pragmatic.

Disruption used to be a relatively rare event 50 years ago: now it's pretty much a daily occurrence, especially at work. The result for many is chronic stress, with all the negative health and performance implications that involves, not to mention time off sick (or worse, presenteeism, where someone is still technically working, but barely functioning).

Those with high mental resilience might face exactly the same disruptive events as their less resilient colleagues, but the outcomes can be very different: more resilient workers are not only healthier, but tend to show better engagement and satisfaction at work, lead more effectively, and develop and learn more readily.

There are many factors involved in resilience – including many of the physical and social wellbeing resources we've just looked at – but there are also some key psychological resources that can be very effectively supported by exploratory writing.

Countering stress

Back in Chapter 5 I introduced agency as one of the foundational principles that makes exploratory writing so effective, and here's where it comes into its own. One of the most common causes of stress is a feeling of powerlessness, the sense that events are happening to us and we have no control. But we're rarely as powerless as we imagine. Exploratory writing creates a space in which we can regain autonomy, a sense of being in charge of our own experience. When we regain the ability to tell our own story, it helps us feel that we can cope with external events more easily.

Reducing negative self-talk

This is another common cause of psychological distress. When something goes wrong, we often assume it's somehow a reflection on us. The Chimp starts jabbering: 'If only I was more organized/cleverer/better connected (delete as appropriate), this would never have happened.'

Left unchecked, this kind of self-critical self-talk can easily spiral into energy-sapping, misery-making rumination. The old adage that daylight is the best disinfectant can be applied here: simply by exposing our self-talk to the light, exploratory writing allows us to see the unhelpful cruelty of this inner monologue. Once we've seen it we can challenge it, or simply dismiss it and focus on the elements of the situation that we *can* control and see new possibilities for solutions.

Increasing playfulness

Just as curiosity is a great antidote to fear, playfulness is the natural enemy of stress.[8] As adults, opportunities to play can be hard to come by in an average day – and even when they come along, we're often too self-conscious to take them. Which means the playfulness inherent in exploratory writing, in a safe and private space, can be a powerful tool for resilience. Once you get the hang of thought experiments such as flipping the Chimp (p. 106) or forced metaphors (p. 96), you can use them to playfully subvert a difficult situation or even to turn your catastrophizing into comedy.

Sensemaking for wellbeing

Remember sensemaking? It's one of the foundational skills of exploratory writing that you met back in Chapter 6, and one of its most useful applications is as a tool to support wellbeing.

When nothing out of the ordinary is happening, our brains coast along. Most of us manage most days with a loose, unregulated set of scripts and assumptions that require little of us and serve us pretty well most of the time. These are habits of mind, and we give them as little thought as the decision about which shoe to put on first each morning. When things are going pretty much as we expect, there's no requirement for us to engage in explicit sensemaking.

But when something unexpected, new or disruptive happens, the old ways of thinking are challenged. That can result in a Chimp-driven negative psychological experience (anger, grief, denial), or it can lead to a Human-led more conscious attempt to make sense of the new experience. No prizes for guessing which is the response most likely to enhance wellbeing.

In everyday life, there are two main ways in which we engage in sensemaking: in our own thinking and in conversation with others. Exploratory writing provides a third, perhaps even more helpful option, as it forces us to articulate our thinking while at the same time allowing us to explore different ideas and their implications without being swayed by others' agendas, judgements or assumptions.

Karl Weick, author of *Sensemaking in Organizations*, noted that writing can play an important role in sensemaking at work: 'there has been an explosion of self-conscious writing about writing styles as tools of persuasion... what most have missed is the use of writing as a tool for comprehension.'[9]

Sensemaking isn't always a simple process. There's rarely a single, clear narrative we can construct quickly to help us understand and accommodate new experience and thereby restore our equilibrium, unless you take the lazy approach: 'Que sera, sera,' perhaps, or 'My horoscope told me to expect arguments today.'

Part of the reason for this is that as we saw in the town hall exercise back in Chapter 7, there are multiple ways of understanding experience, and there are multiple selves within us offering competing narratives about what just happened.

Apart from the psychoanalyst's couch, there aren't too many places in the modern world where we're safe to explore these multiple aspects of ourselves. Most of the time, we're expected – indeed, we expect ourselves – to offer a coherent view. When someone asks me what I think about something, they expect one opinion which expresses my stance on the matter. The reality of course is that various parts of me might have very different opinions.

Let's put this into a real-world scenario. Imagine you're in a meeting; it's just before lunch, the meeting is dragging on, and the marketing director has just proposed a change of tactics. The MD asks you: 'Do you agree with that suggestion?' You say, 'Yes'. The decision is made, the meeting ends, and you're left feeling dissatisfied and cross with yourself, but you don't quite know why. That night you have a row with your partner and don't sleep well.

That's what it looks like on the outside. On the inside, it went more like this:

> *'Do I agree with that suggestion?'*
>
> *Impatient, Hungry You: 'Yes, whatever, just get on with it. I wonder what the quiche of the day is?'*
>
> *Socially Anxious You: 'I wonder what people are expecting of me here? Should I agree or not? Should I offer an opinion? What will X think if I disagree?'*
>
> *Politically Motivated You: 'If I say yes to this, Y will be more likely to support the idea I'm pitching next week.'*
>
> *Thoughtful You: 'It doesn't feel right, but I can't explain why.'*

At normal conversation speed, Thoughtful You doesn't get much of a look-in. But taking a few minutes to do an exploratory writing sprint to explore that uneasiness allows Thoughtful You to get to the bottom of that instinctive response. Even just a few minutes spent alone with a sheet of paper over lunch can be enough to allow Thoughtful You to come back into the room and ask to revisit that decision, potentially saving the company from an expensive mistake as well as increasing the chances of you having a more pleasant evening with your partner and a better night's sleep.

In fact, simply recognizing that multiple responses and narratives are possible is important for our wellbeing. It frees us from the tyranny of first thoughts and reminds us that there are always options, even when we can't see them at first glance, and we are rarely as powerless as we think.

Self-coaching

This process of sensemaking through exploratory writing is essentially self-coaching, so it stands to reason that we can make it more helpful, and more powerful, by putting some coaching structure around it. Yes, simply allowing ourselves to tell a story is useful since it forces us to find words and construct meaning. But reflecting thoughtfully on the stories we find ourselves telling elevates this from helpful to potentially transformative. For example…

One simple technique for self-coaching is to set yourself a coaching-style question as a prompt for your regular exploratory writing sprint. Think of a significant project, conversation or task you've completed recently, and use your writing sprint to reflect on it using one or more of the following prompts, or feel free to use your own:

'What went well?'

'What would I do differently if I were tackling that again?'

'What was the most challenging aspect of this, and why was that?'

'How did I decide on that course of action?'

'How did I get in my own way?'

'What's the main lesson I learned from this?'

Another helpful coaching practice that you can use to support your own wellbeing is noticing and challenging limiting beliefs. Once you're in the exploratory writing habit, you'll notice patterns of thought that have previously been invisible. Take any recent sprint and read back over it, looking for a sentence beginning 'I always…' or 'I never…' or 'I can't…', and there's a good chance you'll find that a limiting belief is lurking within it. Find an interesting one now, or generate one by simply completing the sentence 'I always…' as quickly as you can as often as you like, and examine it in a fresh writing sprint. You could ask yourself:

'Is this ALWAYS true? When is it not true?'

'What evidence is there for this belief?'

'What assumptions is this based on?'

'Is there a different/more helpful way of seeing things?'

Even if you're lucky enough to have access to a great coach, getting into the habit of self-coaching is an invaluable skill if only because no coach is on call 24/7.

Mindfulness

I've left mindfulness until last for a number of reasons. There's no doubt that it's an important aspect of wellbeing and mental health, but the word is almost criminally over-used and seems to resist definition. Most people agree at least that it has something to do with slowing down, with being fully in the moment, being self-aware rather than self-conscious, and separating ourselves from our thoughts in a way that allows us to examine them – not, in fact, unlike the experience of engaging in exploratory writing.

Yet the practice that is most commonly associated with mindfulness in most people's minds is not writing, but meditation, and this is where I struggle.

I am willing to accept that meditation is beneficial – in fact, I'd be a fool to pretend otherwise, given the weight of scientific evidence – but the fact is that I am not good at it. I get bored, frankly, and I find it hard to keep my attention focused. If you are like me, it might help you to know that you're not alone and also that not being a natural meditator does not mean you are condemned to an unexamined life.

Mindfulness does not equal meditation. In fact, people have been using different activities to practise mindfulness for many years.

Robert Pirsig's classic *Zen and the Art of Motorcycle Maintenance* was one of my favourite books as a teenager. The connection in the title between mystical eastern spiritualism and something as mundane as fixing a motorbike captured my imagination. And of course, as Pirsig notes: 'The real cycle you're working on is a cycle called yourself.'[10] I'm no philosopher, nor am I a biker. But for me, exploratory writing is what motorcycle maintenance was to Pirsig: a place I find myself.

I'm not the only one to have made this connection. Peter Elbow describes his idea of 'zen' as 'the peculiar increase in power and insight that comes from focusing your energy while at the same time putting aside your controlling self'.[11] Which is as good a description of freewriting as I can imagine. And Megan Hayes subtitled her book *Writing and Happiness* as 'The everyday zen of writing things down'.

For me, exploratory writing is a more powerful tool for mindfulness than meditation because it provides a focal point that holds me in the moment and gives me space to explore it.

It turns out that I'm not the only one for whom this is the case. According to productivity expert Francesco D'Alessio: 'Meditation is an effective solution, but not as effective as journaling. Journaling trumps meditation when it comes to researched scientific benefits and a way forward for people suffering from anxiety and depressive disorders.'[12]

(Yes, I know he says 'journaling', but that's just shorthand for a form of exploratory writing, in my book – and this is my book.)

Free from the pressure to perform, you can use exploratory writing to inhabit the present moment more fully, without judgement, bringing all your senses to the task and deepening your awareness. It's a great way to lift you above the maelstrom when you feel stressed or anxious.

Mindfulness has its roots in spirituality, so it's not a great stretch to think of exploratory writing in those terms, too. I've often thought that when I first discovered exploratory writing, in my

desperate 3am moment, my writing wasn't so different to the kind
of anguish expressed in the Psalms:

> Have mercy on me, Lord, for I am faint;
> heal me, Lord, for my bones are in agony.
> My soul is in deep anguish.
> How long, Lord, how long?[13]

I like to think that David had a similar instinct to me in his
long dark nights of the soul: he turned to the page to express his
anxiety, setting down his thoughts and feelings before his God
with searing honesty, and in the process finding comfort and
renewing his faith.

Whatever your faith, or even if you have no faith at all, it's worth
keeping this principle in mind: there's a spiritual dimension to our
lives which can be hidden under day-to-day concerns, but which
is harder to deny in the 3am moments.

Writing can be an invitation to respond to that, to pour everything
out to an unshockable deity who is big enough not only to take
whatever grief, guilt, anxiety or pain we can throw at them,
but also big enough to help us gain a new perspective. It's no
coincidence that many of the most powerful Psalms are known as
'songs of ascent', used by pilgrims approaching Jerusalem, but also
metaphorically reflecting a looking upwards in faith:

> I lift up my eyes to the mountains—
> where does my help come from?
> My help comes from the Lord,
> the Maker of heaven and earth.[14]

There's evidence to show that prayer is beneficial to our mental
health,[15] and this externalization and expression of anxious

thoughts is likely to be part of the reason for that, as well as the empathetic benefits of praying for others. You might prefer to think of this as meditation, rather than praying: in many traditions, there's not much difference between them.

That's a lofty note on which to end this section of adventures, but don't stop here.

The page is even bigger than you think...

Part 3

Going further

Congratulations – by now you're a seasoned explorer. I hope that you've enjoyed the writing adventures of the last section. Remember that all the exercises set out here are simply suggestions to get you started on your OWN adventures – feel free to adapt as you see fit, or even ignore those prompts completely and try something different.

The focus of this book is on using writing as a tool for personal exploration and development in life and work. But before we finish, here are some ideas for going beyond: beyond what you might traditionally think of as writing, beyond yourself and outwards into the world, and beyond the end of this book…

Chapter 12
Beyond words

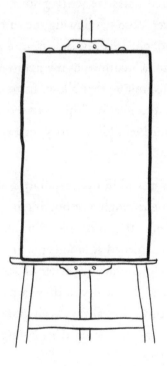

When we think of writing, we think first and foremost of words. But in this chapter we're going to be thinking about non-lexical mark-making. Or, as you're probably more used to thinking about it, drawing.

Drawing? I hear you say: I thought this was a book about writing?

Well, yes. But why be so binary? Drawing, writing, it's all just using the page in the cause of sensemaking. One of the reasons I'm so passionate about using pen(cil) and paper rather than a computer keyboard for exploratory writing is that you can flip effortlessly between lexical and non-lexical marks as your thinking requires. But if you're not used to 'drawing' your thoughts, you might want some convincing as to why it's worth your while, as well as some ideas on how to go about it.

A standard text-based narrative writing sprint takes a basically linear route, however loose – following the thread of a thought, if you like. But thought isn't always linear, especially if you're not neurotypical (not a 'neurmo', as my neuro-atypical daughter puts it…), so any technique that allows us to capture thoughts in ways that show the relationships between them in a more spatial way is a valuable addition to your exploratory writing skillset.

Years ago, when I was still in the corporate world, I was sitting with my MD talking through a resourcing issue that had come up in my department. After a couple of minutes of discussion, he took his notepad, turned it landscape, and started drawing boxes and arrows. He caught my flicker of surprise and said: 'I was 50 before I realized that if you drew a problem you could solve it in half the time.' I've always been grateful he taught me that lesson in my early 30s, rather than letting me figure it out for myself decades later.

Humans are strongly visual creatures: we absorb visual information hundreds or possibly thousands of times faster than written text, and we tend to remember it better too. Adding visual techniques into your exploratory writing practice allows you to access your whole brain, right as well as left hemisphere, and can help you be more creative, identify connections, patterns and relationships between elements, get more clarity about your ideas, and also communicate those ideas more effectively when you're ready to start sharing them.

This is not about creating great art. 'I can't draw' is no excuse: I'm not asking you to channel Picasso in his Blue Period. Having said that, just as writing like nobody's watching helps you be free-er with your ideas, drawing without anyone peering over your shoulder offering an opinion is a liberating experience too. (You might even discover a talent for it, in which case I'd like commission from your first gallery sale, please.) But even if you can't draw the curtains, you CAN put ideas into boxes and draw lines to connect them, and that may be all that's required to give a fresh creative boost to your thinking. Thinking visually means thinking differently about your ideas, and that opens up a whole world of possibilities.

Convinced? Then let's start with the simplest of all visual techniques, and one you're almost certainly already familiar with: mind maps.

Mind maps

The mind map is one of the most popular and useful visual techniques of all. The term was coined by Tony Buzan, but these sorts of radiant diagrams have been around as long as people have been thinking onto paper.

You can use a mind map for pretty much anything – I wouldn't start anywhere else when planning a book, blog post, presentation, course… you name it. They're also great for chunking down big goals and projects into their component parts so you can stop being overwhelmed and actually get started.

Let's start with the basics. A mind map is simply a hierarchical radial diagram, with the topic you're focusing on in the middle of a page and the main themes of that topic radiating out from it as nodes, each in turn linking to subordinate nodes of related ideas.

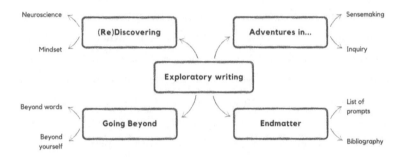

My guess is that you are already very familiar with the basic mind map, and you may even have a favourite software tool. But there are advantages to starting with a hand-drawn mind map, even if you're proficient with an online tool. Here are just a few reasons why:

- The kinaesthetic dimension of using pen on paper activates your brain more fully than typing on a keyboard,[1] which can make you more creative.
- There's something powerful about having a new mind map sitting on the desk, wall or whiteboard for a day or two – it gives you multiple opportunities each day to expand it by capturing new thoughts, or finding new connections.
- It's frictionless – no irritating keyboard shortcuts to learn – meaning your full focus can be on the ideas themselves rather than mastering the software.

- It's available instantly – you can grab a pen and a napkin or old-skool back-of-an-envelope wherever you are when inspiration hits.

So let's try it. Pick a topic that's on your mind – it could be a project, a problem to be solved, or simply an interesting idea you'd like to spend more time with. And then find the biggest piece of paper you can – A4 will do, A3 is better, and if you can lay your hands on a flipchart sheet or roll of decorator's lining paper, fantastic – lay it out in front of you, write the topic you want to explore in the middle, set your timer for six minutes and mind-map away!

Afterwards, take a moment to reflect. How does this more visual technique differ qualitatively from the exploratory writing techniques you've been exploring so far? What happened to your energy? How did your brain work differently? How could you use that more visual technique alongside the tools you've already discovered?

Graphic organizers

Mind maps are just one of a set of tools loosely called graphic organizers. Some of these will be very familiar to you if you've ever had to present annual results in a PowerPoint presentation – bar charts, pie charts, organizational hierarchies; others will be familiar from books and articles you've read – tables, charts and diagrams.

We're used to thinking of these as ways of organizing data post-hoc, once we're clear on what we're saying, as a tool for communication.

But graphic organization is also invaluable for exploratory writing, helping you get clear on the ideas themselves by capturing them in ways that help you understand the relationships between concepts and also generate new connections.

Doing all of these justice would fill a book in itself, so I'm going to focus on just a few that I've found particularly useful for exploratory writing purposes. And I'm starting with my absolute hands-down favourite: the 2 x 2 matrix, also known as the 'magic quadrant' (no exaggeration, in my opinion).

2 x 2 matrix

The idea here is simply to select two variables, which when you put them together along two axes generate four quadrants or options.

One of the most famous is the Eisenhower matrix, originally developed by General Dwight Eisenhower and popularized by Steven Covey in his book *The 7 Habits of Highly Effective People*.

In this example, the two variables used are:

1. whether something is important or not;
2. whether it's urgent or not.

And Eisenhower applied a strategy for each quadrant:

Not urgent/Not important: Delete.

Urgent/Not important: Delegate.

Not urgent/Important: Decide – plan to do it

Urgent/Important: DO IT NOW!

It's a simple, helpful framework to help you assess what's in front of you every day.

Another (much less famous, for now) 2 x 2 matrix is the one I created to classify business writing in the early days of my exploratory writing thinking:

	Internally focused	Externally focused
More clarity	**EXPANDING**	**EXPOUNDING**
Less clarity	**EXPLORING**	**ENGAGING**

It may not have the traction of the Eisenhower matrix – yet – but it was massively helpful for developing my thinking, and it also helped me explain my ideas to people. You'll notice that I express these as a continuum rather than as binary options, which I find is usually more realistic.

When I'm engaging in exploratory writing I'm squarely in the bottom left of the bottom left-hand box: the ideas are unclear and the writing is just for me. As an idea takes shape and I do more and more specific writing sessions around it, I move up into the top left-hand quadrant, where I'm clearer in my own mind about what it is I'm trying to say. Usually I'm simultaneously moving from the bottom left to the bottom right-hand quadrant as I engage trusted other people in 'socializing' the idea, getting feedback and getting them interested and invested in it too. And finally, at some point I'm ready to put the idea out into the world: the book you're currently reading sits up in the top right-hand quadrant – maximum clarity (I hope) and reaching readers I don't yet know (hello!).

You can plot pretty much any kind of business writing on these quadrants. One benefit of organizing my thinking like this was that I realized the importance of the lower right-hand quadrant – how we engage others to help us develop our thinking when our ideas are still unclear – which I hadn't fully articulated before.

Another useful output from this exercise was that it forced me to come up with a word to describe each quadrant – this was the origin of the term 'exploratory writing'.

Ready to have a go at creating a 2 x 2 matrix of your own? First, a disclaimer: this might work brilliantly, or it might not. If it doesn't, that's OK: we're just exploring here, and even if it's a dismal failure you've only lost six minutes. (But I think it might surprise you.)

Again, pick a live issue for you, your leadership style or professional philosophy, a concept you struggle to explain to clients, anything, really, and begin by choosing your two axes – these can either be binary like Eisenhower's (urgent/not urgent) or a continuum like mine (more or less clarity).

As with all forms of exploratory writing, it's less useful to sit around thinking about how to start and more useful just to start, so just draw a quick 2 x 2 box and start trying things out – if the first one doesn't work quite right, try another. It's highly unlikely you'll get to a finished article in just six minutes, but it's VERY likely that you'll move your thinking along and get a helpful insight or two, and hopefully also a sketch that you can refine into something more polished in the future.

If you are really stuck, take a step back. Take a few moments to use one of the 2 x 2 matrix examples above – the Eisenhower matrix or the business writing matrix – and apply it to your own stuff to get a feel for how they're used in practice. Once you're clearer on the principle, you may find ideas for using the model come up over the coming days and weeks.

Don't worry if you find this exercise hard: remember that this is not about getting the 'right' answer or a high score; it's about expanding your thinking toolkit. But in any case take a moment to reflect on the experience of using a visual model: how was it helpful? How was it challenging? How might you develop your embryonic matrix in the future?

Fishbone diagram

Another useful graphic organizer to help support exploratory thinking is the fishbone diagram, which was developed by Professor Kaoru Ishikawa in the 1960s as part of his work on quality control.

This is a mind map with a suit on. A standard mind map lets you meander all over the place – indeed, that's the whole point of it – the fishbone diagram provides a structure for a more rigorous investigation of something, usually a problem you want to fix. It's great for project management and business analysis, but works just as well in an exploratory writing practice, where I like to flip it to reverse-engineer solutions rather than diagnose problems.

However you plan to use it, the principle is the same: you begin by creating the head of your fish. This is, like the centre of your mind map, the topic under investigation. It might be a problem that you want to understand better so you can avoid it happening again: in the example here it's a missed deadline. That goes on the far right of your landscape sheet of paper, and you draw a long horizontal line backwards across the page from that to form the spine of the fish.

Now comes the magic: you identify the major contributing factors to that outcome and list them as branches off that central spine of the fish. It's helpful to use categories for the main branches here – in this example you can see people, method, measurement and so on. Each of these become headings at the end of long straight branch lines, and then you can start to unpack them, creating horizontal lines off each branch with the specific elements that are contributing causes to that overall issue. Under 'people' in this diagram, for example, contributing causes include a micromanaging boss and an absent secretary. (Sounds like the plot of a plausible office-based drama, doesn't it? I think the squeaky chair will turn out to have a pivotal role.)

This is a really useful tool as it stands for problem solving, and by all means go ahead and use it that way if you have a problem that needs solving. But for this exercise I'm going to suggest a twist, transforming it from a serviceable graphic organizer into a bit of pure magic, which is to flip it into a tool for dreaming forward rather than analysing backwards.

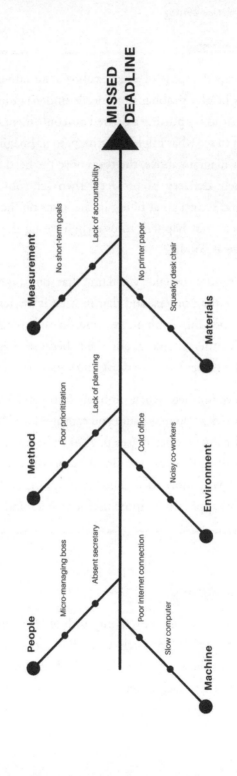

Draw the spine of a fish as above, but rather than making its head a problem that needs understanding and fixing, instead try putting a desired outcome there and then work backwards to see what might contribute to it. Imagine for example that in the diagram above, the text above the head of the fish had read: 'timely delivery of project'. Then set your timer for six minutes and have a go at filling in the items on the branches that would make that happen, reverse-engineering the outcome you want to see, if you like.

Whichever route you take, you'll find that some branches are easier to complete than others, and that in itself is interesting. It might be worth spending a bit more time on the spindlier branches; maybe ask other people about them because that might reveal some of the things that you don't know you don't know.

Once you've finished, you'll probably find you have a number of actions and ideas, so make sure you capture those. You could even use the Eisenhower matrix (see p. 134) to help you prioritize and action them! And reflect too on the process: was it more or less helpful to have a more structured visual approach? When – if ever – might this approach be more useful than a mind map?

Concept diagrams

The last set of models we're going to look at in this section is a broad, very flexible, infinitely extensible group: simple concept diagrams that show what the elements of any given topic are and how they relate to each other.

I'm going to suggest three different flavours to get you started –
process diagrams, cycle diagrams and relationship diagrams – all of
which overlap to some extent. (And remember we're thinking here
about lightweight tools to support early-stage exploratory thinking,
not the more complex analytical or presentational tools that you
might be familiar with if you've ever worked with a business analyst.
Keep telling yourself: there's no wrong way to do this. These are
intended as springboards rather than templates to copy exactly.)

Process diagrams

Process diagrams are a simple linear way of capturing what the
key stages are and the order in which they come, and you can add
more description as you see fit.

I know this looks laughably simple. But the point is that even to
come up with a simple sequence like this you have to clarify in
your own mind what those key stages are, and what they're called,
which in itself can be a valuable process. And when it comes to
communicating your ideas to other people, showing them the
overall process before you dive into the detail is hugely helpful
because it orientates them, making it easier for them to absorb
and retain the information.

Cycle diagrams

A variation on the basic linear process diagram is the cycle diagram,
which is used to represent more iterative processes. I've included

a cycle diagram I used in a recent presentation to talk about the publishing process; notice how marketing is quite literally central to the entire process.

You can zhuzh up a basic cycle in all sorts of ways – cycles within cycles, sequences of cycles, entry and exit points to break the loop – whatever you feel captures your concept most usefully.

Relationship diagrams

The last type of concept diagram we're going to look at in this section is the relationship diagram. Whereas both process and cycle diagrams attempt to capture the flow of a process, relationship diagrams focus more on the way that conceptual elements relate to each other.

One of the most famous, of course, is the pyramid, as used in Maslow's hierarchy of needs – and I have a favourite slightly irreverent internet take on that.

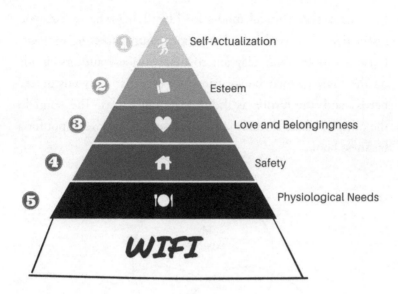

The pyramid shows a progression from the base to the apex, each higher level accessible only once the one below it is in place. It is useful to express the idea of dependence and increasing complexity or refinement.

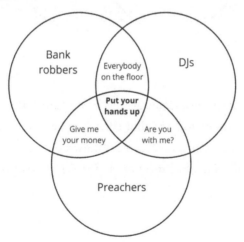

Another useful classic is the **Venn diagram**, which again lends itself beautifully to memes; I've included one I particularly like.

But this is also a useful model for identifying what makes you distinctive when you're thinking about your marketing message. I use a simple Venn diagram to help business authors decide on the topic of their book, using 'my expertise', 'my customers' needs', and 'the future' as the overlapping circles. The point in the middle, where all three circles intersect, is the sweet spot for a business book.

Custom models

While these classic models are great starting points, the possibilities for riffing on them and creating entirely new custom models are infinite. As an example, here's a more illustrative model, developed by Becky Hall in her beautiful book *The Art of Enough*.[2]

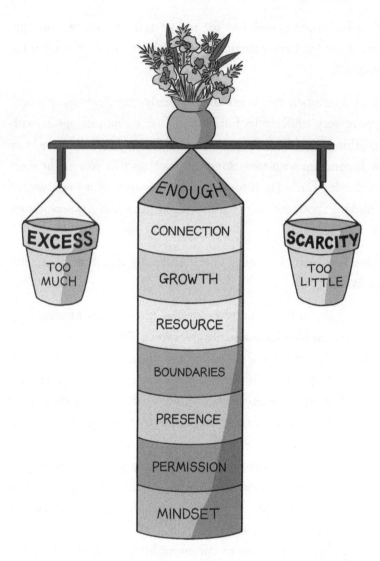

You can see that this model sets out the key components of her concept of Enough and how they come together to create a balance between scarcity on the one hand – feeling that you're not enough – and excess on the other – feeling overwhelmed. It's a lovely demonstration of a graphic organizer developed from an analogy (see p. 155), and it also serves as a memorable visual table of contents.

So what might it look like for *you* to develop your own unique visual model? Let's walk through the process before you try it for yourself.

And remember, this is exploratory, early-stage, ugly-baby stuff:[3] you're very unlikely to finish your first six-minute sprint with anything you'd be willing to share with the world. But you may well come up with something that has legs that you might want to develop further in future, or at the very least with a new way of thinking about the issue (which is all we can ask of any exploratory writing session).

This isn't easy. So why bother? There are two reasons, in my opinion:

1. As you've already discovered, the process of sketching out your ideas visually gives you a different perspective to that of writing them out in a linear way. Not necessarily better, just different, and in the exploratory phase you want as many different ways of understanding your material as possible, because each new angle you try will show you something new and interesting. Using existing models is helpful, but developing your own takes you to a whole new level of clarity, and it means you're not compromising or squashing your ideas to make them fit an existing model.

2. When it comes to communicating your ideas to other people, being able to show them what you mean visually is massively more impactful and effective than trying to describe it in words. And if you can create a distinctive model that you can copyright and share, and which other people use and share with a nod to you, you have developed a distinctive piece of intellectual property in your business, which has real value.

(That second reason is important, but putting too much emphasis on it at this early stage can make you too self-conscious, which isn't helpful. For now, simply focus on the here-and-now benefits of using this as part of your exploratory writing practice: if a useable model emerges, so much the better.)

So how do you go about creating a unique visual model? I'd argue there are four stages, which can be shown nicely in a process diagram (of course).

IDENTIFY THE CONCEPT ▸ IDENTIFY THE ELEMENTS ▸ IDENTIFY THE RELATIONSHIPS ▸ TRY OUT MODELS

The first step is to decide what it is that you want to create a model for. Hopefully by this stage you'll have some ideas to get you started from the exploratory writing exercises you've already done. That's the easy bit.

Now the real work starts: you need to brain-dump the elements that your model will need to include, for example the processes, stages or concepts. As with most things in life, apply the Einstein principle: as simple as possible but no simpler.

You can do this by scribbling on paper, of course, but I recommend using post-it notes as it makes it so much easier to move the elements around when you come to the next stage, which is identifying the relationships between them. This is where the magic happens, and is probably the stage that will take the longest. You have to think about the order of things, their dependencies and their interactions. This is probably also where you'll come up with the insights that will move your thinking forward, and you'll almost certainly have to revisit the second step and add in or rename elements as you go.

Once you have a rough model at the end of that stage, it's time to test it out, first with yourself – does it make sense? Do you like it? Does it get you excited? Because if it doesn't get you excited, it's going to be hard to sell it to anyone else.

And once you have something that you're happy with, you can test it out on some supportive but critical friends: do they get it? If you have to explain it in detail, it's not working well enough yet, but you won't know which bits work and which don't until you try it out on someone who doesn't know what you know. The curse of knowledge is real: we can't see our specialist area as a learner because we can't unknow what we know, so we need to find people who can take that perspective on our behalf.

Ready to have a go at creating a concept diagram of your own? You can use a timer for this if you wish, but you might find it easier to go with the flow. Once you're clear on the concept you want to illustrate, simply brain-dump onto paper – or better still onto post-it notes – what elements need to be included in your model. Then look them over – which are the key ones? Can any be collapsed together? What type of elements are they: processes, concepts, roles, questions, conditions, or something else?

You now have a pile of more or less well-defined elements to work with, so the next step is to play around with how they might fit together. Is the overall shape linear, circular, spiral, or a pyramid or grid? Is there a hierarchy of elements, or different tracks for different conditions? Is there an underlying metaphor you can riff with, like a pipe or flower? The next step is simply to play around with those elements to see what emerges!

What you have in front of you at the end of that process almost certainly won't be a finished model, but it's a starting point, and I hope that you'll continue to iterate and improve it until you're ready to try it out in the wild.

If you've never used visual thinking in this way before, I hope you found it energizing and also insightful. Graphic representation can make us understand ideas more deeply and see connections we hadn't noticed before. And being comfortable experimenting with diagrams like this can supercharge your exploratory practice; the simple act of translating your ideas into a visual representation can't help but enrich and expand your thinking.

Another benefit of getting comfortable with visual thinking in your exploratory writing practice is the fact that a picture is indeed worth a thousand words when it eventually comes to communicating your ideas to others (we'll be thinking more about this in the next chapter). I'm not exaggerating when I say that developing distinctive intellectual property models like this can transform a business – Eric Ries's *The Lean Startup* would never have grown into the movement it has become, for example, without his beautifully simple build/measure/learn cycle diagram.[4]

If you begin developing models at the early stage of your thinking, you have a great head start here. And the good news is that they don't have to be complex.

Economist Kate Raworth, author of *Doughnut Economics*, shared with me how her simple but powerful 'doughnut' doodle – a circular band representing the safe and just space for humanity bounded at its outer edge by an 'ecological ceiling' of sustainability and at its inner edge by a 'social foundation' of human wellbeing

– transformed the way that people understood her ideas about balancing scarcity and excess by making them visual:

> You could just take the same words that are in the picture. You could write health, education, food, water, climate change, biodiversity loss. You could just write those as two lists and everybody would shrug and say, 'Yeah, I've heard of all of those issues before.' But draw it as a circle, and label them in the circle, and the image itself is doing the work, and people start saying, 'Oh, oh, my goodness. I've always thought of sustainable development like this. I've just never seen the picture before. Now I can have conversations and ask questions I felt I couldn't ask.' It really astounded me the power of imagery to open up our thinking.[5]

Developmental biologist John Medina claimed that if we hear a piece of information, three days later we'll remember only 10% of it. If that same information is paired with an explanatory image, that proportion increases dramatically to 65%.[6]

This is a good point to acknowledge the elephant in the room: we began by dismantling the idea that the page is always and only a stage, and we've focused on the power of writing just for ourselves. But the essence of writing is communication. There comes a time when we need to get comfortable with the page-as-a-stage and communicate our ideas to others. Can exploratory writing help with this too?

I think you're going to like the answer…

Chapter 13

Beyond yourself

I hope that in my enthusiasm for exploratory writing, I've not given you the impression that I think writing for others has no value.

Because that of course is tosh, and the fact that I've taken the time and trouble to write this book proves it.

In fact, I believe that writing for others is a key business skill. It's easy to forget in a world where the book charts are dominated by fiction that writing began as a business tool. The earliest forms of writing we have are not epic poems but the records of Sumerian merchants, dating from around 5,000 BCE: as Daniel Levitin points out, 'all literature could be said to originate from sales receipts'.[1]

And writing continues to be foundational to business today. It's how we communicate within an organization to get things done; how we communicate who we are, what we do and why it matters to our customers; and how we're discovered and evaluated online. Whether you're an entrepreneur putting together sales copy and blog posts, a manager writing reports or a senior leader preparing an all-company strategy presentation, being able to write effectively makes success more likely. And as with everything in life, practice can't help but help.

David Ogilvy, the father of advertising, wrote a famous memo to his staff in 1982 which began thus: 'The better you write, the higher you will go in Ogilvy and Mather. People who think well, write well.'[2] And he went on to point out that good writing is a skill like any other, and needs to be learned and practised. (The memo is a great summary of advice for business writers – indeed ALL writers – and it's well worth a read, not least because it walks its own talk so perfectly.)

So will regular exploratory writing help you with the expository writing you may have to do in the course of your work day? Damn right it will. Here's how.

Getting started

First of all, exploratory writing can help you beat the terror of the blank page. At the risk of stating the obvious, if you're going to write something worth reading, you need to start by actually writing. But it's easy to be struck dumb by 'page-fright', imagining a host of critical readers waiting to judge your words. Which is why, as Peter Elbow points out: 'So much writing time and energy is spent *not* writing: wondering, worrying, crossing out, having second, third and fourth thoughts... [freewriting] helps you learn simply to *get on with it* and not be held back by worries about whether these are good words or the right words.'[3]

A six-minute exploratory writing sprint won't give you the final script for your TED talk or the annual letter to shareholders. But it WILL help you get started, and provide the raw material you can shape into something presentable over time.

Once you're comfortable simply applying your bum to the seat and your pencil to the page with nothing more than a vague idea or even just a question in your mind, you'll never suffer from writer's block again.

Building confidence

I hope you've already discovered that exploratory writing builds confidence generally by providing evidence, time after time, that you have all the resources you need within you for sensemaking, creativity, problem solving and more. Most people fairly quickly start to become more confident in their ability to generate and express ideas, if not immediately, then after some wrangling. But it's also the case that simply writing more helps you write better.

As with any skill, the more often you do it the more fluent and fluid you become. As you read back over the raw mess of your writing sprints, you begin to notice what 'works', the phrases and images that ring true and seem to jump off the page. And this growing sense of being able to articulate yourself can't help but make you feel more confident when you're writing for others. Yes, you might still want to ensure that Grammarly has your back on the apostrophes, but the really important part of any piece of writing is the value of what you're actually saying to the reader and the way in which it lands with them. And exploratory writing gives you an unfair advantage on both those counts.

Generating better content

One of the main reasons to engage in exploratory writing is that it allows you to uncover something that's worth saying.

It's trivially easy to be a passive recipient of other people's content – this is idea *consumption* and doesn't benefit anyone other than yourself. It's relatively easy to share other people's ideas along with your initial reaction to their opinion: this is idea *curation* and can have real value. But when you take a few minutes in an exploratory writing sprint to unpack and sort your thoughts, it becomes surprisingly easy to break through to the next level, which is what marks out thought leaders: idea *creation*. The process of writing is one of the most reliable and powerful methods we have for moving our thinking forward. So rather than sitting staring at the quarterly report and desperately trying to come up with an engaging message for shareholders using the latest tech firm's statement for inspiration, take it offline and go exploring first; then bring your most useful insights back and work them up into something fit to be seen.

Now let's look at two specific exploratory writing techniques that lend themselves particularly well to writing that's ultimately intended to land well with other people.

Analogy

In Chapter 9 we looked at how you can make metaphors work for you by surfacing those hiding below the surface and consciously generating new ones to create new insights. Once you've found a metaphor that works particularly well, you may want to use it out in the world, to help explain things to other people. This is where analogy comes in, and exploratory writing can be helpful here too.

Analogy is essentially a metaphor on steroids: it's a more conscious usage, expanding the comparison to draw out the connections and in the process helping someone understand the thing being described more fully.

So for example, if I were to say that you are 'processing' this information as you read, I'd be using a metaphor which you might barely notice: using the language of computing to talk about how your brain is functioning. To turn that into an analogy, I'd draw it out more fully and in a more explanatory way: 'Just as a computer receives input from the outside world through its interfaces and processes it into binary code, the brain converts sense information into neural activity for processing.' Explaining something new in terms of something familiar helps us understand it more quickly – though it can also be misleading if we take the analogy too far. (There's a lot of pseudo-science about our 'off-switch', for example.)

Very often as business writers we're concerned simply with putting across the facts. And sometimes that's exactly what's required. But equally, sometimes we want to surprise the reader, engage them, make them remember what we're saying, help them understand something that's hard for non-specialists to grasp, and that's when we turn to analogy.

To explore this for yourself, try developing a metaphor that you discovered in your Chapter 9 work and found particularly helpful into an analogy that might help others understand the topic better. If you're really stuck, here are a few examples to try:

- Leadership is like hosting a dinner party because...
- Organizational culture is like climate because...
- Starting a company is like building a house because...

This exercise takes you to the borders of exploratory writing – for the first time, I'm asking you to write with a potential reader in mind. It's worth spending a few moments reflecting on that. How did that change how you approached the task? How can you convert the freedom and energy of exploratory writing into content that's useful for others? Is there an opportunity for you to experiment with analogy in your work or life today?

Telling better stories

We saw in Chapter 2 that storytelling is an irresistible impulse of the human brain. It's also a key business skill, precisely because of that neurological quirk: creating emotional connection helps us cut through the noise and engage readers' full attention whereas dry facts simply slide in one ear and out of the other.

But storytelling is a craft, and like any craft it demands practice and skill. Regular writing won't turn you into a master storyteller but it will certainly help build the necessary muscles. Some of the techniques in this book, such as empathy in Chapter 6, have demanded that you write imaginatively, creating stories to explore possibilities and make sense of experiences. So far, the primary purpose of these has been to help you think more effectively, but an important secondary benefit, and the one we're going to focus on here, is the difference it will make to your ability to tell a story well.

Practising empathy and perspective taking in particular will help you connect with your readers, which in turn makes it more likely that they will connect with you.

Let's try a writing sprint aimed at capturing someone else's perspective specifically for the purposes of better communication. Choose someone that you need to be able to influence persuasively: it could be a potential customer or client for whom you need to write convincing sales copy, a leader or potential investor to whom you want to pitch an idea, a partner who's less than convinced about your holiday plans… you get the idea.

Set your timer for six minutes and write about the relevant situation as a story *from that person's perspective*. What do they most care about? What are they worried about? What's the worst that could happen, as far as they're concerned, and what's the potential upside? What do they need to hear from you? Using storytelling to imaginatively identify with that person on the page will help you communicate with them far more effectively when it's time to engage with them in real life.

And finally, let's look at exploratory writing as the means to a very different kind of end – not better business communication or better relationships, but simply for the sake of writing itself.

Creative writing applications

The very first time I heard about freewriting – the most foundational skill in the exploratory writing toolkit, which we explored in Chapter 6 – was in Julia Cameron's *The Artist's Way*, where she introduced Morning Pages as one of her foundational practices of creativity.

Morning Pages are simply that: three sides of legal-size (A4, roughly) paper, 'strictly stream-of-consciousness', written long-hand every morning, for your eyes only. Cameron explicitly differentiates the practice from what we think of as 'writing':

> [They] are not meant to be art. Or even writing… Writing is simply one of the tools. Pages are meant to be, simply, the act of moving the hand across the page and writing down whatever comes to mind.[4]

When Cameron first devised the practice for herself, having retreated to New Mexico to get her head together after the disappointment of another failed screenplay, she found to her surprise that her meandering scribbles became the springboard for a novel. She now teaches it primarily as a tool for unblocking and unlocking creativity.

Many writers routinely use this sort of technique – not necessarily first thing in the morning – as a way of blasting through writer's block and self-doubt. If you've been part of a writers' group, you may well have tried it yourself.

But this focus on creativity, writing for its own sake, is not just for novelists, poets and screenwriters: it can help anyone who needs to communicate through writing do so with more impact.

Peter Elbow, former director of the Writing Program at Amherst University and author of *Writing with Power* and *Writing without Teachers*, discovered this technique for himself out of desperation, facing a long-standing writer's block that began under the pressure to perform as a scholarship student at Oxford University.

But he soon discovered that freewriting was more than just a way of blasting through writer's block. It actually produced better writing in the long run because the words that emerge when you're 'out of control' often have more power and energy than those you might choose if you were more consciously crafting the piece:

> It's not just a way to get by, there are actually virtues in the language… sometimes I can tell when the writer has worked too hard at choosing the words… there is a lot of skill there but it doesn't have the flow, it doesn't have the energy… when a writer gets rolling and the words just come there's something magical about the language and the thinking that happens.[5]

What's true for screenwriters, novelists, academics and others who have to write for a living is also true for those of us who write reports, memos, or even just WhatsApp messages. Exploratory writing can not only help us become more creative and overcome the fear of the blank page; it also helps us express our ideas with more energy and clarity.

And who doesn't want that?

Chapter 14

Beyond today

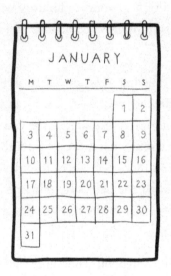

When the grand British Victorian explorers returned home, the second phase of the expedition began: they would give talks at the Royal Society recounting their adventures, hand over new specimens to the Natural History Museum for researchers to examine, and carefully transfer seeds to the Botanic Gardens at Kew for propagation and analysis. (All too often they also handed over other peoples' priceless cultural treasures to the British Museum, but that's a topic for a whole new book...)

They didn't, in other words, simply go and explore and then come back home and do nothing with what they'd discovered.

How will you use what you discover on your exploratory writing expeditions?

Capturing the discoveries

In the basic toolkit in Chapter 3, I suggested that a notebook was a 'nice-to-have' addition to your exploratory writing supplies, as a way of noting down insights and actions in a more presentable way.

I decided against making this an essential bit of kit, but I do strongly recommend you have *some* way of capturing the discoveries from your micro-explorations as you go. You will need to be very selective about what makes it from the white-hot mess of the A4 sheet to this more permanent record. An explorer might hack 99 paths through the bamboo: only one of them, it turns out, was a firm, safe path to the river, and that's the one that is captured on the map.

You might find that a notebook is not quite right for you, which is one reason why I decided to designate it as 'optional'. Personally, rather than a notebook, I have three options for capturing insights from a writing sprint, depending on what they are: my private blog (which is essentially an online journal) for aha moments; my Trello to-do list for actions; and a separate Trello board for ideas for future content creation (for example, LinkedIn articles or podcast episodes).

How you capture the outputs from YOUR writing sprints might be entirely different, depending on the tools you already use to capture ideas and what you intend to do with them. But do think about this before you start: notes to self on post-it notes are NOT a scalable solution.

Once you have a way of capturing your insights, particularly those that go beyond simple to-do actions, how can you make the most of them in life and work from this point on? I believe that the power of in-the-moment, extemporized exploratory writing realizes its full value when it's combined with the regular discipline of reflective practice, which provides a model for converting the insights it generates into endless, iterative self-development.

Reflective practice

Reflective practice as an academic and professional tool builds on the work of David Kolb, who famously set out his model of experiential learning as a cycle with four phases:

1. **Concrete experience** – something happens that demands a non-routine response or challenges your skills.
2. **Reflective observation** – this is the bit of most interest to us from an exploratory writing perspective. Classic questions you might ask yourself at this stage include: what worked? What failed? Why did that happen? Why did I do what I did, and why did others behave the way *they* did?
3. **Abstract conceptualization** – at this point you move on from reflecting on what happened to think about how you might do things differently in the future: how could you improve your response? What resources and ideas might be helpful?

4. **Active experimentation** – you take your new understanding and ideas about how to do things differently, and you put them into practice. And then the cycle begins all over again as you translate your ideas into concrete experience and reflect on the outcomes.

This is an excellent theory, familiar to every MBA student, but when was the last time someone chatted to you about it at work? Most of us, most of the time, bounce from concrete experience to active experimentation and back. I remember working once alongside a harried project manager who was nearly in tears because she simply couldn't persuade the project sponsor and leadership team to make time for an evaluation meeting at the end of each project phase. This reflection was seen as a luxury they simply didn't have time for, and so the project continued to teeter on the edge of disaster and deadlines continued to be missed. (She quit, and who can blame her.)

Our typical *modus operandi* can be summed up by Douglas Adams's acid observation: 'You live and learn. At any rate, you live.'[1]

Donald Schön put his finger firmly on the issue when he described our daily work environment as 'the swampy lowlands'[2] – when we're down there on the ground day by day it's hard to see the big picture; there are no helpful signs to guide us and certainly no paths. We rely, he concluded, on two types of reflection:

1. **Reflection-in-action**, which is done on the hoof in the swamp, by trial and error.
2. **Reflection-on-action**, when we retreat to the high ground and reflect on what just happened. This is the core of reflective practice, and it's where learning and development can happen most effectively.

One place in which reflective practice *is* firmly embedded is academia. If you've studied recently, you'll know that reflecting on your assignments and projects is a core part of your learning experience. Gillie Bolton points out that reflective practice isn't just about improving performance; it's a personal and social responsibility:

> Reflective practice can enable discovery of who and what we are, why we act as we do, and how we can be much more effective… The search for solutions, leading to yet more pertinent questions and more learning, leads to unsettling uncertainty: the foundation of all education.[3]

Finding the time for this kind of reflective practice isn't always easy, but it is *always* useful. In 2014, researchers from Harvard, Paris and North Carolina attempted to quantify the benefits. They worked with a team of customer service agents in training, encouraging one group to spend 15 minutes at the end of each day reflecting in writing on how the day had gone and the other to spend 15 minutes practising their skills. The reflecting group improved their performance by nearly 25% over their practice-only peers. The researchers concluded that: 'the performance outcomes generated by the deliberate attempt to articulate and codify the accumulated prior experience are greater than those generated by the accumulation of additional experience alone.'[4]

I'm delighted to hear from my children that reflective practice is now a key part of school life too – perhaps the next generation of professionals will bring this habit with them into the workplace of the future. With the levels of uncertainty and change they're likely to be facing, they're certainly going to need it.

Sadly, it's unlikely that anyone is supporting you to embed reflective practice into your own life and work – but that's OK: your new exploratory writing skills mean you can now do it for yourself.

Conclusion

So, is it going too far to call exploratory writing magic? Personally, I don't think so. What else is the right word for a process that makes the invisible visible, that can transform a hopeless situation into an opportunity for growth, and scattered fragments of ideas and impressions into a workable whole?

For me, the most magical part of exploratory writing is the potential it represents. No matter how badly the day has gone, how mired we are in failure or frustration, the blank page represents a new start in a clear space whenever we need it.

I wrote much of this book in Gladstone's Library, a beautiful light space of warm wood and cool stone, lined with thousands of books and where the silence is broken only by an occasional cough or the shuffling of papers. When someone enters the reading room, you can see a physical change: they pause, breathe, slow down. The space, beauty and peace of the room, its quiet atmosphere, create a sense that this is a place for doing work that matters, for focus, for thought.

Sadly, not all of us have access to a room like that whenever we need it. But a blank page? That's always accessible. I have discovered that I can make the scruffiest blank page the mental equivalent of that beautiful quiet space. For a few minutes at least, I can centre, focus, explore the vast library of my mind without interruption, or just breathe, if that's what's required.

So if you've got this far and haven't yet tried it for yourself, now is the moment. Go grab a piece of paper and a pen. I'll wait.

Ready? Take a moment to appreciate the blank page in front of you and what it represents.

Nobody's looking over your shoulder. This is your space. Let it be whatever you need it to be right now, and just write.

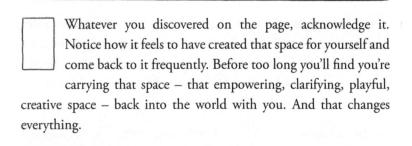

Whatever you discovered on the page, acknowledge it. Notice how it feels to have created that space for yourself and come back to it frequently. Before too long you'll find you're carrying that space – that empowering, clarifying, playful, creative space – back into the world with you. And that changes everything.

List of prompts

*I*n addition to the exercises you've already encountered in this book, here are some useful prompts to turn to whenever you need a little inspiration for your exploratory writing session. Many of these have been road-tested around The Extraordinary Business Book Club virtual campfire for our group writing sessions, and have never failed to elicit useful ideas and insights. Others were suggested by members of the Club and other contacts on social media. They're in no particular order, so just pick one at random and get going!

Remember that these are just jumping-off points, and they may be miles away from where you land – that's the whole point! – so don't worry about 'answering' the question; just see where it takes you.

If you have a favourite prompt of your own, do share it with me: alison@alisonjones.com. Or bring it along to the virtual campfire one Friday, or share it in The Extraordinary Business Book Club Facebook group!

- What story am I telling myself about this?
- What's another way of looking at this?
- What would I say to a friend here?
- What's most interesting about this?
- What question do I need to ask myself right now?
- What does success look like today?
- If I could have a coaching session with X, what would they say?

- If I were a journalist covering my business, what story would I focus on?
- What would happen to my business/job if I couldn't type tomorrow?
- What have I learned since I wrote this? (e.g. when reviewing the About page on your website or your biography)
- What's the quietest part of me saying right now?
- What advice do I give others that I really need to take myself?
- What's bringing life today?
- To me, visibility means...
- What can I see, hear, smell, touch, taste right now? [A lovely grounding exercise]
- At my best, I...
- Where can I replace perfection with progress this week?
- Dear x-year-old me... (write a letter to your younger self, particularly at a time of need or celebration – what do/did you most need to hear?)
- Who could help with this?
- What do I really want here?
- I think the reason I don't know the answer to this is...
- What do I need to let go of/say no to today?
- What's the truest sentence I can write today?
- What small step will make the biggest difference today?
- What memory isn't helping me and how can I reimagine it?
- If I were writing from the heart and not the ego about this, what would I say?
- My superpower is...
- The difference I make to this project/meeting/relationship is...
- My 'game-changer' today is...
- If I had two hours of 'brave time' this week [i.e. when your 'courage' score was temporarily boosted by a factor of 10], what would I do?

- What unconscious assumptions/biases are stopping me seeing the full picture here?
- When I look back on this week, I want to say...
- If I could do that again, I would...
- Right now, I am feeling...
- Right now, what's working is...
- This week, I am no longer available for...
- Here's what people need to know...
- In what way does this thought/action help/hinder me becoming the person I want to be?
- Right now, the best part of me is saying...
- Whose perspective would be valuable here?
- If I could focus on just one thing in my work/life/ relationships today, it would be...
- Why am I the right person for this task?[1]
- How can I move the needle just 1% today?
- What's my biggest advantage here? (Follow up: And am I making full use of it?)
- What am I most grateful for today?
- What can I celebrate right now?
- I used to think... Now I think...[2]

What now?

You're at the end of this book, but it's just the start of your exploratory writing adventure, which I hope will last the rest of your life.

I'd love to hear what you discover along the way. Please drop me a line at alison@alisonjones.com and let me know where your exploring has taken you.

That's the email address to use if you'd like to book a talk or workshop to introduce the power of exploratory writing into your organization, too.

And if you'd like more support with your own exploratory writing practice, why not join my WriteBrained online course? This 28-day exploratory writing adventure, with a new prompt delivered to your inbox each morning and a short video explaining a little more about each day's task, is a great way to kickstart a daily exploratory writing practice, and there's a supportive Facebook community with which to share your discoveries and reflections. Join here – www.exploratorywriting.com – and get 50% off with this code: EXPLORIAMUS.

The page is waiting for you. What will you turn it into today?

Notes and references

Introduction

[1] For more on this story, see my TEDx talk 'Let's Rethink Writing' (https://youtu.be/59sjUm0EAcM).

Chapter 1

[1] The Extraordinary Business Book Club podcast, Episode 245 (http://extraordinarybusinessbooks.com/episode-245-sorting-the-spaghetti-with-dave-coplin/).

[2] The Extraordinary Business Book Club podcast, Episode 318 (http://extraordinarybusinessbooks.com/episode-318-the-power-of-regret-with-daniel-h-pink/).

[3] The Extraordinary Business Book Club podcast, Episode 308 (http://extraordinarybusinessbooks.com/episode-302-writing-it-all-down-with-cathy-rentzenbrink/).

[4] The Extraordinary Business Book Club podcast, Episode 11 (http://extraordinarybusinessbooks.com/ebbc-episode-11-the-space-within-with-michael-neill/).

Chapter 2

[1] Nelson Cowan, 'The magical mystery four: How is working memory capacity limited, and why?' *Current Directions in Psychological Science* 2010;19(1), 51–57. https://doi.org/10.1177/0963721409359277

[2] Yuval Noah Harari, *Sapiens: A Brief History of Humankind* (Vintage, 2015), p. 150.

[3] Cal Newport, *Deep Work: Rules for focused success in a distracted world* (Piatkus, 2016).

[4] Steve Peters, *The Chimp Paradox: The mind management programme to help you achieve success, confidence and happiness* (Ebury, 2012).

5 Angela Duckworth, *Grit: The power of passion and perseverance* (Vermilion, 2017), p. 189.

6 Center for Decision Sciences, Columbia Business School, 'Want to know what your brain does when it hears a question?' Available from www8.gsb.columbia.edu/decisionsciences/newsn/5051/want-to-know-what-your-brain-does-when-it-hears-a-question (accessed 23 January 2022).

7 This term is from psychologist Antonio Damasio's theory of consciousness, and has been widely used elsewhere. See Damasio, 'Investigating the biology of consciousness', *Philosophical Transactions of the Royal Society* 1998;353(1377), 1879–1882.

8 Gordon H. Bower & Michal C. Clark, 'Narrative stories as mediators for serial learning', *Psychonomic Science* 1969;14, 181–182.

9 Taken from David Foster Wallace's commencement address at Kenyon College, 2005. You can read the full text here: https://fs.blog/david-foster-wallace-this-is-water/ (accessed 10 August 2022).

10 Michael Neill, *Living and Loving from the Inside-Out*. Available from www.michaelneill.org/pdfs/Living_and_Loving_From_the_Inside_Out.pdf (accessed 10 August 2022).

Chapter 3

1 Grace Marshall, *Struggle: The surprising truth, beauty and opportunity hidden in life's sh*ttier moments* (Practical Inspiration Publishing, 2021), p. 52.

2 Carol Dweck, *Mindset: The new psychology of success* (Ballantine Books, 2007).

3 Edgar Schein, *Humble Inquiry: The gentle art of asking instead of telling* (Berrett-Koehler Publishers, 2013).

4 Sir Ernest Shackleton, *South: The last Antarctic expedition of Shackleton and the Endurance* (an edition of Shackleton's own account, published by Lyons Press, 1998), p. 77.

5 Quoted in Tor Bomann-Larsen, *Roald Amundsen* (The History Press, 2011), p. 99.

6 Gillie Bolton with Russell Delderfield, *Reflective Practice: Writing and professional development*, 5th edition (Sage, 2018).

[7] B. J. Fogg, *Tiny Habits: The small changes that change everything* (Virgin Books, 2020).

[8] James Clear, *Atomic Habits: An easy and proven way to build good habits and break bad ones* (Random House Business, 2018).

Chapter 4

[1] Quoted in Arianne Cohen, 'How to quit your job in the great post-pandemic resignation boom', *Bloomberg*, 10 May 2021. Archive available from https://archive.ph/qJC76 (accessed 5 July 2022).

[2] Jim Harter, 'U.S. employee engagement holds steady in first half of 2021', *Gallup*, 29 July 2021. Archive available from https://archive.ph/guoOV (accessed 5 July 2022).

[3] As reported for example in UK government figures for 2021: Health and Safety Executive, 'Work-related stress, anxiety or depression statistics in Great Britain, 2021', 16 December 2021. Available from www.hse.gov.uk/statistics/causdis/stress.pdf (accessed 10 August 2022).

[4] John Howkins, *Invisible Work: The future of the office is in your head* (September Publishing, 2021), p. 131.

[5] Ibid, p. 139.

[6] Gary Klein, 'Performing a project premortem', *Harvard Business Review*, September 2007. Available from https://hbr.org/2007/09/performing-a-project-premortem (accessed 10 August 2022).

[7] 'Thriving at work: The Stevenson/Farmer review of mental health and employers', 2017. Available from https://assets.publishing.service.gov.uk/government/uploads/system/uploads/attachment_data/file/658145/thriving-at-work-stevenson-farmer-review.pdf (accessed 10 August 2022).

[8] Mind, 'Mental health facts and statistics', 2017. Available from https://web.archive.org/web/20220508130219/https://www.mind.org.uk/media-a/2958/statistics-facts-2017.pdf (accessed 10 August 2022).

Chapter 5

[1] See for example Craig R. Hall, Diane E. Mack, Allan Paivio & Heather A. Hausenblas, 'Imagery use by athletes: Development of the Sport Imagery Questionnaire', *International Journal of Sport Psychology* 1998;29(1), 73–89.

² The Extraordinary Business Book Club podcast, Episode 287 (http:// extraordinarybusinessbooks.com/episode-287-writing-and-happiness-with-megan-hayes/).

³ Dscout, 'Putting a finger on our phone obsession'. Available from https://web.archive.org/web/20220507125042/https://dscout.com/people-nerds/mobile-touches (accessed 10 August 2022).

⁴ Stevie Smith, 'Thoughts about the Person from Porlock' in *Selected Poems* (Penguin Modern Classics, 2002), p. 232.

Chapter 6

¹ The Extraordinary Business Book Club podcast, Episode 312 (http:// extraordinarybusinessbooks.com/episode-312-free-writing-with-peter-elbow/).

² Karl Weick, *Sensemaking in Organizations* (Sage, 1995), p. 128.

³ Collins English Dictionary, definition of 'empathy'. Available from www. collinsdictionary.com/dictionary/english/empathy (accessed 19 August 2022).

⁴ Charles Duhigg, 'What Google learned from its quest to build the perfect team', *The New York Times*, 25 February 2016. Available from www.nytimes.com/2016/02/28/magazine/what-google-learned-from-its-quest-to-build-the-perfect-team.html (accessed 7 July 2022).

⁵ Marcus Aurelius, *Meditations* – quoted in Paul Robinson, *Military Honour and the Conduct of War: From Ancient Greece to Iraq* (Taylor & Francis, 2006), p. 38.

⁶ John Greenleaf Whittier, 'Maud Muller', 1856.

Chapter 7

¹ Leon Neyfakh, 'Are we asking the right questions', *Boston Sunday Globe*, IDEAS section, 20 May 2012. Available from www.bostonglobe.com/ideas/2012/05/19/just-ask/k9PATXFdpL6ZmkreSiRYGP/story.html (accessed 3 August 2022).

² See her excellent TED talk: 'What do babies think?' Available from www.ted.com/talks/alison_gopnik_what_do_babies_think (accessed 10 August 2022).

³ Warren Berger, *A More Beautiful Question: The power of inquiry to spark breakthrough ideas* (Bloomsbury, 2016), p. 24.

[4] Helen Tupper and Sarah Ellis, *You Coach You: How to overcome challenges and take control of your career* (Penguin Business, 2022), p. 11.

[5] @TonyRobbins on Twitter, 27 June 2017. Available from https://web. archive.org/web/20220810175946/https://twitter.com/TonyRobbins/ status/879796310857048064?s=20&t=F05rZAiYz0VzUE3lYgNWwA (accessed 7 July 2022).

[6] The Extraordinary Business Book Club podcast, Episode 287 (http:// extraordinarybusinessbooks.com/episode-287-writing-and-happiness-with-megan-hayes/).

[7] Walt Whitman, 'Song of Myself', section 51 in *Leaves of Grass* (1855).

[8] J. K. Rowling, *Harry Potter and the Prisoner of Azkaban* (Bloomsbury Children's Books, 2014, first published 1999), p. 438.

[9] I first experienced this myself when I undertook Tara Mohr's 'Inner Mentor Visualization', which you can read more about in her book *Playing Big*.

[10] Hal Gregersen, 'Better brainstorming', *Harvard Business Review*, March–April 2018. Available from https://hbr.org/2018/03/better-brainstorming (accessed 10 August 2022).

[11] Edgar Schein's *Humble Inquiry: The gentle art of asking instead of telling* (Berrett-Koehler Publishers, 2013) is a great starting point. He defines 'humble inquiry' as 'the fine art of drawing someone out, of asking questions to which you do not already know the answer, of building a relationship based on curiosity and interest in the other person' (p. 3).

Chapter 8

[1] Sir Ken Robinson, 'Do schools kill creativity?' TED talk, 2006. Available from www.ted.com/talks/sir_ken_robinson_do_schools_kill_ creativity?language=en (accessed 10 August 2022).

Chapter 9

[1] Paul H. Thibodeau and Lera Boroditsky, 'Metaphors we think with: The role of metaphor in reasoning', *PLoS ONE* 2011;6(2), e16782. https://doi. org/10.1371/journal.pone.0016782 (accessed 10 August 2022).

[2] In conversation with The Polymath Perspective, 2014, available here: https://web.archive.org/web/20220810194600/http://

polymathperspective.com/?p=3107 (accessed 10 August 2022). Eno was the co-creator (with Peter Schmidt) of Oblique Strategies, a card deck of random suggestions to inspire artists' creativity, an idea not dissimilar to forced metaphors.

Chapter 10

[1] Clinton Askew, 'The Chimp Paradox – Prof. Steve Peters', *Citywide Financial Partners*, 15 September 2020. Available from www. citywidefinancial.co.uk/the-chimp-paradox-prof-steve-peters/ (accessed 10 August 2022).

[2] Alice Sheldon, *Why Weren't We Taught This at School?* (Practical Inspiration Publishing, 2021).

[3] Alice Sheldon, *Why Weren't We Taught This at School?* (Practical Inspiration Publishing, 2021), p. 68.

[4] The Extraordinary Business Book Club podcast, Episode 318 (http://extraordinarybusinessbooks.com/episode-318-the-power-of-regret-with-daniel-h-pink/).

[5] Elizabeth Gilbert, 'On creating beyond fear', *The Isolation Journals*, 19 November 2020. Available from www.theisolationjournals.com/blog/no-4-on-creating-beyond-fear (accessed 10 August 2022).

Chapter 11

[1] Rachel Dodge, Annete P. Daly, Jan Huyton & Lalage D. Sanders, 'The challenge of defining wellbeing', *International Journal of Wellbeing* 2012;2(3), p. 230.

[2] Mihaly Csikszentmihalyi, *Flow: The psychology of optimal experience* (Rider, 2002, first published 1993).

[3] Sara Milne Rowe, *The SHED Method: The new mind management technique for achieving confidence, calm and success* (Michael Joseph, 2018).

[4] Hayley Phelan, 'What's all this about journaling?' *The New York Times*, 25 October 2018. Available from www.nytimes.com/2018/10/25/style/journaling-benefits.html (accessed 10 August 2022).

[5] James W. Pennebaker & Sandra K. Beall, 'Confronting a traumatic event: Toward an understanding of inhibition and disease', *Journal of Abnormal Psychology* 1986;95(3), 274–281.

[6] Julia Cameron, *The Right to Write: An invitation and initiation into the writing life* (Hay House, 2017), p. 84.

[7] Bruce Daisley, *Fortitude: Unlocking the secrets of inner strength* (Cornerstone Press, 2022), p. xiv.

[8] See for example, Cale Magnuson & Lynn Barnett, 'The playful advantage: How playfulness enhances coping with stress', *Leisure Sciences* 2013;35, 129–144.

[9] Karl Weick, *Sensemaking in Organizations* (Sage, 1995), p. 197.

[10] Robert Pirsig, *Zen and the Art of Motorcycle Maintenance: An inquiry into values* (Vintage Classics, 1991), p. 267.

[11] Peter Elbow, *Writing with Power: Techniques for mastering the writing process* (Oxford University Press, 1998), p. 16.

[12] Francesco D'Alessio, 'The science behind journaling: How the brain reacts', *Therachat*, 28 December 2018. Available from https://blog. therachat.io/science-of-journaling/ (accessed 10 August 2022).

[13] Psalm 6:2-3, New International Version.

[14] Psalm 121: 1-2, New International Version.

[15] For example, a 2009 study showed 'significant improvement of depression and anxiety, as well as increases of daily spiritual experiences and optimism'. Peter A. Boelens, Roy R. Reeves, William H. Replogle & Harold G. Koenig, 'A randomized trial of the effect of prayer on depression and anxiety', *International Journal of Psychiatry in Medicine* 2009;39(4), 377–392, p. 377.

Chapter 12

[1] E.g. Audrey L. H. van der Meer & F. R. (Ruud) van der Weel, 'Only three fingers write, but the whole brain works: A high-density EEG study showing advantages of drawing over typing for learning', *Frontiers in Psychology*, 2017;8 706. They concluded that 'drawing by hand activates larger networks in the brain than typing on a keyboard'.

[2] Becky Hall, *The Art of Enough: 7 ways to build a balanced life and a flourishing world* (Practical Inspiration Publishing, 2021).

[3] This is Pixar founder Ed Catmull's phrase for ideas in their earliest stages, when it's not easy to see their full potential and they're vulnerable to criticism. See Ed Catmull, *Creativity, Inc: Overcoming the unseen forces that stand in the way of true inspiration* (Transworld, 2014).

4 Eric Ries, *The Lean Startup: How today's entrepreneurs use continuous innovation to create radically successful businesses* (Portfolio Penguin, 2011).

5 The Extraordinary Business Book Club podcast, Episode 98 (http://extraordinarybusinessbooks.com/episode-98-doughnut-economics-with-kate-raworth/).

6 John Medina, 'Brain rule rundown'. Available from http://brainrules.net/vision/ (accessed 10 August 2022).

Chapter 13

1 Daniel Levitin, *The Organized Mind: Thinking straight in the age of information overload* (Penguin, 2015), p. 13.

2 Cited in Mark Frauenfelder, 'David Ogilvy's 1982 memo "How to Write"', *Boing Boing*, 23 April 2015. Available from https://boingboing.net/2015/04/23/david-ogilvys-1982-memo.html (accessed 23 January 2022).

3 Peter Elbow, *Writing with Power*, 2nd edition (Oxford University Press, 1990), p. 14.

4 Julia Cameron, *The Artist's Way: A course in discovering and recovering your creative self* (Profile Books, 2020), p. 10.

5 The Extraordinary Business Book Club podcast, Episode 312 (http://extraordinarybusinessbooks.com/episode-312-free-writing-with-peter-elbow/).

Chapter 14

1 Douglas Adams, *Mostly Harmless* (Pan Macmillan, 2009, first published 1992), p. 138.

2 Donald Schön, *Educating the Reflective Practitioner: Toward a new design for teaching and learning in the professions* (Jossey-Bass, 1987), p. 42.

3 Gillie Bolton with Russell Delderfield, *Reflective Practice: Writing and professional development*, 5th edition (Sage, 2018), p. 14.

4 Giada Di Stefano, Francesca Gino, Gary P. Pisano & Bradley Staats, 'Making experience count: The role of reflection in individual learning', *Harvard Business School Working Paper*, No. 14-093, March 2014.

List of prompts

[1] This is an example of what Alisa Barcan calls 'afformations': rather than simply repeating a positive statement to yourself, turn it into a question and let your brain find the answers for itself, e.g. 'Why am I the right person to write this book?' rather than 'I am the right person to write this book'. Yay instinctive elaboration!

[2] Developed as part of the Visible Thinking project at Project Zero, Harvard Graduate School of Education.

Bibliography

Bolton, Gillie with Russell Delderfield, *Reflective Practice: Writing and professional development*, 5th edition (Sage, 2018).

Cameron, Julia, *The Artist's Way: A course in discovering and recovering your creative self* (Tarcher, 1992, new edition Profile Books, 2020).

Cameron, Julia, *The Right to Write: An invitation and initiation into the writing life* (Hay House, 1998).

Clear, James, *Atomic Habits: An easy and proven way to build good habits and break bad ones* (Random House Business, 2018).

Csikszentmihalyi, Mihaly, *Flow: The psychology of optimal experience* (Rider, 2002).

Daisley, Bruce, *Fortitude: Unlocking the secrets of inner strength* (Cornerstone Press, 2022).

Di Stefano, Giada, Francesca Gino, Gary P. Pisano & Bradley Staats, 'Making experience count: The role of reflection in individual learning', *Harvard Business School Working Paper*, No. 14-093, March 2014.

Dodge, Rachel, Annette Daly, Jan Huyton & Lalage Sanders, 'The challenge of defining wellbeing', *International Journal of Wellbeing* 2012;2(3), 222–235.

Dweck, Carol, *Mindset: Changing the way you think to fulfil your potential* (first published 2012, 6th edition, Robinson, 2017).

Elbow, Peter, *Writing with Power: Techniques for mastering the writing process*, 2nd edition (Oxford University Press, 1998).

Elbow, Peter, *Writing without Teachers*, 25th anniversary edition (Oxford University Press, 1998).

Fogg, B. J., *Tiny Habits: The small changes that change everything* (Virgin Books, 2020).

Galef, Julia, *The Scout Mindset: Why some people see things clearly and others don't* (Piatkus, 2021).

Gilbert, Elizabeth, *Big Magic: Creative living beyond fear* (Bloomsbury, 2016).

Gilligan, Stephen & Robert Dilts, *The Hero's Journey: A voyage of self-discovery* (Crown House Publishing, 2009).

Grant, Adam, *Think Again: The power of knowing what you don't know* (W. H. Allen, 2021).

Hall, Becky, *The Art of Enough: 7 ways to build a balanced life and a flourishing world* (Practical Inspiration Publishing, 2021).

Harari, Yuval Noah, *Sapiens: A brief history of humankind* (Harvill Secker, 2014).

Harper, Faith G., *Unf#ck Your Brain: Using science to get over anxiety, depression, anger, freak-outs, and triggers* (Microcosm Publishing, 2017).

Holland, Cara, *Draw a Better Business: The essential visual thinking toolkit to help your small business work better* (Practical Inspiration Publishing, 2018).

Janzer, Anne, *The Writer's Process: Getting your brain in gear* (Cuesta Park Consulting, 2016).

Kahneman, Daniel, *Thinking, Fast and Slow* (Penguin, 2012).

Levitin, Daniel, *The Organized Mind: Thinking straight in the age of information overload* (Penguin, 2015).

Kolb, David A., *Experiential Learning: Experience as the source of learning and development* (Prentice Hall, 1984).

Milne Rowe, Sara, *The SHED Method: The new mind management technique for achieving confidence, calm and success* (Michael Joseph, 2018).

Mohr, Tara, *Playing Big: For women who want to speak up, stand out and lead* (Hutchinson, 2014).

Newport, Cal, *Deep Work: Rules for focused success in a distracted world* (Piatkus, 2016).

Pennebaker, James W. & Sandra K. Beall, 'Confronting a traumatic event: Toward an understanding of inhibition and disease', *Journal of Abnormal Psychology* 1986;95(3), 274–281.

Pennebaker, James W. & Joshua M. Smyth, *Opening Up by Writing It Down: How expressive writing improves health and eases emotional pain* (Guilford Press, 2016).

Peters, Steve, *The Chimp Paradox: The acclaimed mind management programme to help you achieve success, confidence and happiness* (Ebury, 2012).

Peters, Steve, *A Path Through the Jungle: Psychological health and wellbeing programme to develop robustness and resilience* (Mindfield Media, 2021).

Pirsig, Robert, *Zen and the Art of Motorcycle Maintenance: An inquiry into values* (Vintage Classics, 1991).

Progoff, Ira, *At a Journal Workshop: Writing to access the power of the unconscious and evoke creative ability*, revised edition (Inner Workbooks series, Jeremy P. Tarcher, 1992).

Roam, Dan, *Back of the Napkin: Solving problems and selling ideas with pictures* (Portfolio, 2008).

Schein, Edgar, *Humble Inquiry: The gentle art of asking instead of telling* (Berrett-Koehler Publishers, 2013).

Schön, Donald, *Educating the Reflective Practitioner: Toward a new design for teaching and learning in the professions* (Jossey-Bass, 1987).

Schön, Donald, *The Reflective Practitioner: How professionals think in action* (Ashgate, 1991).

Sheldon, Alice, *Why Weren't We Taught This at School? The surprisingly simple secret to transforming life's challenges* (Practical Inspiration Publishing, 2021).

Tupper, Helen & Sarah Ellis, *You Coach You: How to overcome challenges and take control of your career* (Penguin Business, 2022).

Raworth, Kate, *Doughnut Economics: Seven ways to think like a 21st-century economist* (Chelsea Green Publishing Company, 2017).

Rushdie, Salman, *Imaginary Homelands: Essays and criticism 1981–1991* (Granta, 1991).

Weick, Karl E., *Sensemaking in Organizations* (Sage, 1995).

Acknowledgements

There are many hundreds of people whose insights and encouragement have shaped this book, and to whom I am profoundly grateful. However, as I don't let other Practical Inspiration authors write ten-page acknowledgement sections, I probably shouldn't allow myself that luxury either. So this is an incomplete, insufficient list, but it's better than nothing.

Thanks first to the Practical Inspiration Publishing team and our design and production partners Newgen Publishing UK for their patience and good humour as I missed deadline after deadline (and especially Shell for conjuring up writing time out of an impossibly full diary and protecting it for me fiercely). Working with these people is everyday magic indeed.

Thanks to Alison Gray, development editor extraordinaire, for helping me unearth the structure that had eluded me for so long, to copy-editor Katie Finnegan for polishing the final manuscript into shape, and to Mary Ala for the lovely 'page' illustrations.

This book's first expression was as a beta version of the WriteBrained course, so a huge thank you to all those who stepped up to try it out and give feedback: Anne Archer, Kathryn Bishop, Lyn Bromley, Joy Burnford, Alison Coward, Linda Duff, Felicity Dwyer, Gill Ereaut, Krista Powell Edwards, Susan Haigh, Becky Hall, Gary Hosey, Nikki Huddy, Honey Lansdowne, Craig McVoy, Grace Marshall, Susan Ni Chriodain, Clare Painter, Akhil Patel, Chris Radford, Lucy Ryan, Beth Stallwood, Ben Wales and George Walkley, and particularly to

Helen Dann, Sheila Pinder and Alice Sheldon whose expert insights and warm encouragement first helped me believe this idea had legs.

Thanks too to all those who've met with me around The Extraordinary Business Book Club virtual campfire over the years, for their openness and generosity, wisdom and savvy, and mostly just for being great company on a Friday afternoon.

A shout-out to my fabulous 12-week-warrior-women group – Bec Evans, Liz Gooster, Grace Marshall, Cathy Rentzenbrink and Laura Summers – for their phenomenal insights, support and challenge. Thanks particularly to Bec for her thoughts on structure and for introducing me to Gladstone's Library, where most of this writing was done (and certainly the best bits).

Thanks to all those who suggested additional prompts for the appendix: Alisa Barcan, Jon Bartlett, Kathryn Bishop, Brian Cavanagh, Lisa Edwards, Krista Powell Edwards, Gary Hosey, Martin Klopstock, Aneta Ardelian Kuzma, Deb Mashek, Katy Murray, Roy Newey, Jo Richardson, Lucy Ryan, Naomi Lynn Shaw, Tricia Smith, Antonia Taylor and Lyanna Tsakiris.

Finally, thank you to all my guests on The Extraordinary Business Book Club podcast for helping me explore writing so thoughtfully and generously, to all those who listen, and to you, reader, because writing may begin with exploration but it doesn't end there – ultimately, it's all about connection.

About the author

Alison Jones, MA, MBA has been a pioneer of publishing since 1992, from her days as an editor with Chambers Harrap and Oxford University Press to Director of Innovation Strategy at Macmillan, before setting up Practical Inspiration Publishing in 2014.

Today she helps business leaders write and publish exceptional business and self-development books, and champions the value of both reading and writing in business.

She is the host of The Extraordinary Business Book Club podcast, a judge for the Business Book Awards, and author of the bestselling *This Book Means Business: Clever ways to plan and write a book that works harder for your business* (2018) as well as a variety of slightly random reference works. Her TEDx talk 'Let's Rethink Writing' has over 80,000 views on YouTube, and she regularly gives talks and workshops to organizations on using exploratory writing for better outcomes at work.

She is a runner, reader, writer, and enthusiastic advocate for all three, mostly fuelled by faith, tea and peanut butter.

To find out more, visit www.alisonjones.com.

Index